AMERICA'S HEARTLAND

To   7-03

Uncle Phil

From

Joe & Mary

AMERICA'S HEARTLAND

ROBIN LANGLEY SOMMER

BARNES
&NOBLE
BOOKS
NEW YORK

Page 1: A neon cowboy welcomes visitors to Jackson, Wyoming.

Page 2: Whitewater rafting on the Salmon River near Peach Springs, Indiana.

Page 3: America's national bird has symbolized majesty and strength since ancient times. In Greek mythology, the eagle carried the thunderbolts of all-powerful Zeus. The Bald Eagle was adopted as a national symbol by the United States in 1782, when it was first used on the Great Seal.

For the dedicated men and women of our police forces, fire departments, emergency rescue teams, and others who risk their lives daily to keep us safe and secure.

This edition published by Barnes and Noble, Inc., by arrangement with Saraband

2002 Barnes & Noble Books

Copyright © 2002 Saraband (Scotland) Ltd.

Library of Congress Cataloging in Publication Data available

ISBN: 0-7607-3224-8

Printed in China

10 9 8 7 6 5 4 3 2 1

Editor: Sara Hunt
Contributing Editor: Simon Saunders
Photo Editor: Deborah Hayes
Art Editor: Nikki L. Fesak

CONTENTS

Introduction: This Land is Your Land   6

1.   From Many, One: Building Communities   12

2.   Rural Scenes and Folkways   90

3.   This American Life   150

4.   This Beautiful Land   224

Index   302

INTRODUCTION:
THIS LAND IS YOUR LAND

The story of America, still unfolding, is a vivid diorama of lights and darks, dreams and harsh realities, high ideals and human fallibility, evolving since prehistoric times in a landscape of unique beauty and dramatic diversity. When human beings—probably Asian hunters tracking game across a land bridge that once stretched from Siberia to Alaska—set foot on this primeval continent, its extent was undreamed of. Over a period of thousands of years, such bands formed various tribes whose lifeways were determined largely by the geography and climate of the regions where they settled. These first Americans were the explorers, settlers, and builders of communities from the Pacific Northwest to the Eastern Woodlands, which stretched from the Atlantic coast to the Mississippi River. (This area was so heavily forested when European settlers arrived that it was said that a squirrel could cross the entire region without once touching the ground.)

While our first people, then, came from the east, countless migrations from the west began with the voyages of Christopher Columbus, whose glowing reports of the New World he had "discovered" in the service of Spain inspired successive waves of Europeans to seek the earthly paradise he described: "the best and most fertile and temperate...and excellent that is in the world." Land-hungry commoners, refugees from religious persecution, seekers of gold and glory, zealous missionaries—all followed in his wake. Over the centuries after 1492, they continued to come, braving countless hardships and dangers to make a new life in an unknown land. They settled the Atlantic mainland and spread thence to the Appalachians and the Midwest, the Great Plains, the Rocky Mountains, the Southwest, and the Pacific coast. Thus Americans became known as a westering people, irresistibly drawn by the desire to see what lay beyond the next wooded ridge, intractable desert, or rushing river. Frontiersman Daniel Boone

expressed it with simple eloquence when he recalled that "It was on the first of May, in the year 1769, that I resigned my domestic happiness for a time, and left my family and peaceable habitation on the Yadkin River, in North Carolina, to wander through the wilderness of America, in quest of the country of Kentucke." In so doing, he found the Cumberland Gap through the Appalachians, opening up the first great American West.

However, as historian Alvin M. Josephy, Jr., observed in 1986: "It is important to recognize that to the people who moved on, there was always, in each generation, a new 'West.' Moreover, wherever the West was at any point in time, it never stood alone in history, detached from the main centers of life—which had once been frontiers themselves—but was a profound contributor to the culture and historic course of its age. In short, although the many Wests...lay along the outer fringe of civilization and conjure up vivid images of their own, they were always an integral part of the essence and flavor of our total national experience." This observation remains valid today, as we see immigrants and visitors from new sectors of the global community enriching American life and culture with their unique contributions. Thus this volume is not merely a pictorial history, but a vivid and appreciative overview of our many-faceted society, seen from multiple perspectives. It focuses on four themes: Building Communities, Rural Scenes and Folkways, This American Life, and Our Beautiful Land. A wealth of photographs accompanies each chapter, illustrating our rich multiethnic heritage as embodied in art and architecture, occupations, recreation, exploration, transportation, and other human endeavors. At the same time, the panorama of the land itself—vibrant cities, fruitful farms and orchards, and unspoiled wilderness preserved for future generations—unfolds before us.

Opposite: America's open roads through spectacular countryside symbolize the spirit of freedom and adventure that pervades the national culture.

The landmarks described here include shrines of worship, government, and regional history, as well as natural treasures like the Cascade and Rocky Mountains, the Grand Canyon, the Mississippi and Columbia Rivers, and the Outer Banks of North Carolina, described by the British seafarer Arthur Barlowe in 1584 as a region of "such plenty…that I think in all the world the like aboundance is not to be founde." Those who came after him were equally struck by the natural features of the New World, and their contagious enthusiasm brought ever-growing numbers of immigrants to carve homesteads and plantations from the wooded East Coast and to fish its waters. Settlers from the Netherlands left their imprint in the form of brick townhouses in what is now New York City and its boroughs, and Dutch Colonial barns and farmhouses with the double-sloped gambrel roof adopted from English neighbors. Swedish and German settlers built log barns and cabins that would become identified with life on the frontier.

Spanish influence is still apparent in Florida, where St. Augustine was founded in the sixteenth century, and in the Southwest, where conquistadors and settlers from Mexico mingled with the native peoples and later with Anglo immigrants from the eastern United States. Adobe construction centered around cooling patios is typical of the homes and churches here, and cowboys still round up cattle for transport with the help of skillful "cow ponies" and lariats, or lassos, to single out steers for branding and separate cows from calves when the young animals have been weaned. California, larger than life, has a breathtaking coastline, extensive farmlands, giant sequoia forests, the punishing heat of Death Valley, and myriad attractions from star-struck Los Angeles to legendary San Francisco, climbing the hills from its waterfront to the heights overlooking San Francisco Bay and the Golden Gate Bridge.

The Midwest takes pride in its pivotal role in building the nation, with many original settlers who emigrated from Germany, French Canada, and the Scandinavian countries. With ax and plowshare, they advanced across this fertile heartland, their progress marked first by small, scattered homesteads and then by tightly knit communities whose members produced rich harvests and raised sturdy livestock. Some of those communities evolved into the great cities that we know today as Chicago, Cleveland, Cincinnati, Detroit, Milwaukee, Minneapolis, and St. Louis, called the Gateway to the West. During the nineteenth century, railroads extended into the region and grain elevators sprang up alongside them to bring produce to other parts of the country. Sturdy barges plied the Great Lakes and the Erie Canal, laden with everything from huge vats of liquid molasses to milled flour and manufactured goods. Michigan's two peninsulas have shorelines on four

Below: A man's best friends wait patiently for their owner at the Diamond Inn Bar, Denio, Nevada.

Above: Inside an all-American hardware store in Jackson, California.

of the five Great Lakes. The Upper, or northern, Peninsula stretches from its southwestern border with Wisconsin 320 miles east between Lakes Superior and Michigan toward windswept Ontario, Canada. The Lower Peninsula runs north from borders with Indiana and Ohio between Lake Michigan on the west and Lakes Huron and Erie on the east. The two peninsulas are separated by the five-mile-wide Straits of Mackinac that connect Lakes Michigan and Huron.

Farther west is a diverse region of mountains and plains that presented daunting challenges to those who sought to make their way here, from Native American tribes to American settlers. It remains a challenging environment, with record-breaking snowfalls, winter temperatures far below zero degrees Fahrenheit, and intricate canyons of multicolored stone shaped by eons of wind, weather, and erosion. ("Hell of a place to lose a cow," as one laconic farmer remarked.) Tall-grass prairies were laboriously carved into isolated homesteads whose shelters were built from blocks of sod, since timber was so scarce. Ceaseless labor was required to maintain both people and domestic animals in this environment, but settlers were tenacious. They formed close bonds, worshipped together, and helped one another clear stony fields and produce such necessities as warm clothing, soap, candles, and tools. Montana, Nebraska, the Dakotas, Wyoming, and Colorado were gradually, if sparsely, settled before the nineteenth century ended, and provide us with some of the nation's most awe-inspiring scenery and such legendary figures as mountain man Jedediah Smith and his fellow trappers, who found the South Pass through the Rockies to Oregon and California. Today, the region is a mecca for skiers, hikers, campers, and others who enjoy the outdoors.

Right: *A tender moment between mother and infant, captured on the streets of New Orleans' French Quarter.*

Opposite: *Jean Dubuffet's artwork* Monument au Fantôme (Monument to the Phantom) *adds an exotic touch to the glass-and-steel environs of Houston's Louisiana Street. Dubuffet was a pioneer of "outsider art," and was associated with such great American artists as Jackson Pollock.*

The Pacific Northwest, one of our last regions to be settled, conjures up images of majestic beauty, ranging from the rugged coast that runs north from Cape Mendocino, California, to the far reaches of Alaska. Here, towns and cities were built along sheltered harbors on the Columbia River system and the irregular coastline of Puget Sound, an arm of the Pacific that penetrates deeply into Washington State and provides access to Alaska via its northern inlets.

The inland waterways of this region are alive with steamships, ferries, tugs, fishing boats, and private craft of every kind. Countless islands, including those in the Strait of Juan de Fuca, comprise a major recreational area, and the area west of the Cascade Range contains thriving cities including Seattle, Washington, and Portland, Oregon. The vitality of Northwestern pioneers can still be felt today, as the region's many attractions draw increasing numbers of both residents and visitors. Far-seeing conservation policies are preserving an irreplaceable wilderness heritage, while rich natural resources—fish, shellfish, timber, agricultural products, minerals—contribute to the booming economy. East of the Cascades, where the climate is drier, Ponderosa pine predominates, and the forests become more scattered, interspersed with meadows. The foothills

gradually give way to the wonders of the Columbia River Basin, where torrential streams have cut deep gorges through a landscape formed by lava and ice flows millennia ago. What could have been a desert due to the relatively sparse rainfall between the Cascades and the Rockies is a rich agricultural area boasting orchards, grain fields, and cattle ranches. Grand Coulee Dam, astride the Columbia, and a number of similar major engineering projects testify to the human influence on fulfilling the promise of this part of the country.

As you turn the pages of this tribute to our native land, it is hoped that you will be inspired to reaffirm your personal and communal commitment to the principles enunciated by our Founders and the legacy of freedom and fellowship hard-won by our predecessors and contemporaries. Each person has an important part to play in making this relatively young republic a force for good, and an exemplar of integrity, in a world that has become increasingly interdependent. As the past flows into and shapes the present from day to day, we have every reason to believe, despite the upheavals inseparable from social change and progress, that our common bonds will prevail over every adversity to maintain and strengthen our honorable place in the community of nations.

FROM MANY, ONE: BUILDING COMMUNITIES

Travelers from other lands may well wonder if they are still in the same country, as America unfolds before them in all its diversity of landscape and community life. The amazing panorama stitched together by roads, railways, streams, and rivers, even the skyways, is so varied that it sometimes seems like many nations in one—and so it is. One could spend a lifetime exploring it, and fill huge archives with its history, art, and legends, but even a week or two spent seeing it with new eyes conveys some sense of its unique beauty and variety.

We Americans find our country endlessly interesting and are forever on the move—from house to house, city to country, state to state. We've been known for that restless urge to see what's beyond the next ridge or bend in the river since the first pioneers pushed past the Eastern mountain ranges to see what was on the other side, and what kind of life might be built there. As a people, we are known for optimism, mobility, and an increasing willingness to merge the best of our many ethnic backgrounds into a diverse but coherent whole.

Regional and climatic differences have played a major role in America's development since pre-Columbian times. The Native American culture groups were as distinctive in their lifeways as the Europeans, Asians, Africans, and others who came later. The Makah of the Pacific Northwest called themselves "people who live on the cape by the rocks and seagulls." Their way of life was shaped by the rainforest at their backs and the sea before them, where they hunted marine mammals, fish, and shellfish. In the Southwest, the Pueblo peoples adapted themselves to the scorching sun, the chill of the desert night, and the need to conserve every drop of water. The lives of the Plains Indians moved to the rhythm of the tall-grass prairie and the buffalo herds.

Opposite: *The Stars and Stripes displayed above the entrance to the Renaissance-style Reading Terminal (1893) in Philadelphia, Pennsylvania, the city in which the Declaration of Independence was signed.*

Below: *The ruins of dwellings built around one thousand years ago by the Anasazi, or "Old Ones," in Frijoles Canyon, in New Mexico's Bandelier National Monument.*

In the warm regions of the Southeast, the Cherokee built extensive villages centered upon their ceremonial mounds, which brought heaven and earth together symbolically. Their streams were filled with fish, and their farmlands were enriched by flooding that formed deltas from which crops sprang abundantly. In the Eastern woodlands of what is now New England and the Mid-Atlantic states, the five tribes of the Iroquois Nation dwelt securely in their longhouses and evolved a form of self-government that was similar in many ways to that of the future national republic. In both co-operation and conflict, the first Americans made an indelible imprint on those who came later, and they continue to do so as they assert their valuable contributions to the nation.

The first English settlers reached the Atlantic shoreline some 400 years ago, making landfall in what is now Plymouth, Massachusetts, and at Jamestown, Virginia. The northern group, which arrived in 1620, comprised dissenters from the established Church of England, who set out on the diminutive sailing ship *Mayflower*. The Pilgrims, as they called themselves, sought freedom of worship in an untried wilderness and a chance to improve their circumstances through trade, farming, and other enterprises. Apparently, they had intended to join the group that had colonized Jamestown in 1607, but were blown off course into what is now New England. After several severe winters, and with the help of friendly Native Americans, they began to adapt to their new environment, building thatched-roofed wooden cottages with gardens fenced to deter straying animals. They learned that their farm animals needed more shelter to survive the severe New England winters, so they constructed three-bay barns, with a threshing floor at the center and hay mows and stables on either side. Their shelters were of the sturdy post-and-beam type familiar from Elizabethan England, with woven sticks covered with mud (wattle and daub) filling the wall spaces between the timber uprights. Hand-split clapboard surfacing provided weatherproofing.

When other English Separatists, the Puritans, heard that their brethren were finding religious freedom and greater opportunities in the New World, despite the difficulties it presented, they took ship and arrived in growing numbers to found communities including Salem and Boston, Massachusetts. Their meetinghouses reflected their austere faith, which rejected the pomp and ritual of the Church of England, which derived from the Roman Catholic Church. There were no altars, images, candles, or incense. Instead, the pulpit was the focal point of their original houses of worship—usually, square wooden structures with hipped roofs that rose to a central cupola. Later, white wooden churches with frontal towers would become identified with the New England Congregationalists. Since their theocratic communities made no distinction between sacred and civil law, these buildings also served for town meetings, where decisions affecting the members were made. In their simplicity, they were similar to the meetinghouses of the Quaker sect, which had been persecuted vigorously in England for its pacifism and rejection of ritual.

The Quakers and the similar faith community called the "Shaking Quakers," or Shakers, also found new homes in colonial America. The Shakers, who were celibate, lived in close-knit

Below: *America's oldest surviving Puritan meetinghouse—the Old Ship Church, in Hingham, Massachusetts, begun in 1681.*

communes and expressed their spiritual ideals in the form of spontaneous liturgical dancing (from which they derived their name) and the production of simple, clean-lined furniture and other handcrafted household goods and herbal remedies. They built notable barns for their livestock, farmed productively, and shared everything in common. Their integrity won the respect of other early New Englanders, and their products were valued for their superior workmanship.

The explorations of Henry Hudson gave the Dutch East India Company an early opportunity to establish colonies in what is now New York State, from the lower tip of Manhattan Island to regions far up the Hudson River Valley. The Dutch were capable traders, builders, and seafarers, as seen in their rapid development of New Amsterdam (New York City) into a bustling port lined with dockside warehouses and commercial exchanges. What is now the nation's best-known financial center, Wall Street, was originally a wall built by Dutch merchants to prevent English encroachment on their domain. Although Dutch hegemony in this part of the New World ended in 1664 with British conquest, Dutch colonial enterprise and building styles had a much longer influence.

Farmers from the Netherlands built sturdy houses of timber and stone with brick veneering, and long house/barns like those of their homeland. Examples may still be seen in Long Island, Staten Island (the Richmondtown Restoration), New Jersey, and upper New York State. Some of the nation's first townhouses were built in New Amsterdam, Albany, and Schenectady, New York. The latter has a fine historic district that preserves examples of these neat front-gabled houses, many of which were two stories high: all were faced with brick to conform to the fire laws. (Wooden buildings in close proximity to one another were subject to disastrous fires that swept through entire blocks, so these laws prevailed widely in the original thirteen colonies.) Similarly, stable fires were prevented by placing smokehouses and blacksmiths' sheds at a considerable distance from the barn, which evolved into a dual-purpose animal shelter and granary in the New World. (In Europe, these functions had rarely been combined under one roof.) Thus an early American proverb stated that "A lamp on the table means death in the stable." Candles and lanterns were never left burning unattended in the barn.

Many early settlers in New England found that farming was difficult in the rocky soil of the

Above: *Mystic Seaport, Connecticut, is a living history museum whose mission is to promote understanding of the nation's maritime heritage. Its attractions include a restoration shipyard, historic vessels, and a planetarium with exhibits on the principles of navigation.*

region, a legacy of the last Ice Age. They turned their hands to new endeavors, including local and overseas trading, whaling, fishing, and commerce in furs with the French in eastern Canada and Native American hunters and trappers. Over time, the rigorous Puritan way of life, as described in Nathaniel Hawthorne's novel *The Scarlet Letter*, alienated newcomers like Roger Williams and Anne Hutchinson, who were expelled from the Massachusetts Bay Colony because they sympathized with the Quakers. During the 1630s, they established the first settlements—notably, Providence—in what is now Rhode Island, where religious freedom became more fully realized. Denominations including the Baptists and the Jews, as well as the Quakers, were welcomed.

Others found a secure haven in Pennsylvania (Penn's Woods), founded by the Quaker William Penn in 1681 under a royal charter. With its principal town of Philadelphia, and its beautiful forested hills and meadows, the colony became a mecca for faith communities including the Mennonites and their offshoot, the Amish, who had been persecuted in Switzerland and the Rheinland. In the New World, they established close-knit family groups that worshipped in one another's houses and farmed the land diligently.

They built connected house/barns on the central-European model, or extensive family farms with houses to shelter several generations, and sturdy bank barns, dug partly into a hillside for protection of the livestock and crops. Generally, a long wooden forebay projected over a masonry base where the animals were housed, and the threshing floor and granaries above were accessed by a ramp for wagons. The so-called Pennsylvania bank barn was emulated as far away as northern New England and eastern Canada.

Much of eastern Pennsylvania is still called Amish country, and the sect has remained loyal to its original customs, foregoing the use of automobiles and electric power in favor of the traditional horse and buggy and farm machinery operated manually rather than with gasoline motors. There are few sights more satisfying than the well-kept Amish farmstead, with its handsome barns painted with colorful hex signs in the Old World manner. Scholars long attributed these designs to a belief that they warded off evil forces (the German word *Hexe* means witch), but the farmers themselves assert that they are purely decorative (or "chust for pretty"). As the eastern frontier opened up, many of the Amish moved into areas of Ohio and Indiana (part of the orig-

Below: *The windmill for pumping water and the absence of electrical lines are clues that this farmstead in New Hope, Ohio, is part of an Amish community.*

inal "Northwest Territory"), where they continued to excel at farming and animal husbandry.

Other immigrants who were attracted to Pennsylvania included Scots-Irish and Germans in need of land, who heard that Penn's colony offered the most humane laws known anywhere in the world. Swedes made the first permanent settlement in adjacent Delaware in 1638, and their distinctive log cabins would become an emblem of the frontier. German settlers arrived afterward, building their homes and outbuildings in a similar style, called *Fachwerk*. Tiny Delaware would change hands several times before it passed to William Penn in 1682, and it remained a part of Pennsylvania until the Revolutionary War. Today, its proud motto is "The First State," since it was the first to ratify the U.S. Constitution.

Another group that soon grew dissatisfied with the rigorous Puritan regime left the Massachusetts Bay Colony under the leadership of Thomas Hooker to colonize the fertile Connecticut River Valley, where many prospered as farmers and merchants, including the itinerant "Yankee peddlers" who brought much-needed goods like metalware, spices, and fabric to isolated communities, carrying news from town to town in the process. Each homestead had to be cleared of virgin for-

est before permanent dwellings were built and crops could be planted. But a strong sense of solidarity was fostered by the interdependence of neighbors, and many small hamlets shared the services of a local blacksmith, barn builder, mason, or master carpenter. Tobacco farming eventually became a lucrative enterprise in this region, as it had in the Virginia colony, and special barns were constructed to dry the huge tobacco leaves on long poles. These barns had few or no windows, and their walls were hinged wooden panels that provided ventilation.

One of New England's best-known forms of vernacular architecture originated as a modified cottage known as the saltbox, because it resembled a medieval salt container. This type of cottage had a lean-to shed built onto the back as a kitchen or bedroom area. The result was a long, north-facing, sloped roof (usually surfaced with hand-split shingles) that shed rain and snow readily and provided protection against strong winter winds. Ideally suited to the climate, this versatile style took on many variations, including the Nantucket Island whaler's house, with a lean-to shed on both sides of the main dwelling. Eventually, the saltbox would be constructed from Atlantic Canada to southern Connecticut.

Farther south, the Virginia colony, after several unsuccessful attempts, began to prosper. Its original palisaded settlement along the James River soon sent outposts into the surrounding countryside, and its milder climate was more conducive to successful plantation farming than that of the colonies farther north. Here, post-and-beam shelters could have less substantial walls, so early houses left much of the framing exposed in the style known as half-timbering. (This is familiar to us today mainly from the Tudor Revival style of the late nineteenth and early twentieth centuries, in which stucco exteriors were banded by exposed woodwork that had a decorative rather than a structural function.) The fireplaces in these houses were served by stone chimneys that protruded from an end wall rather than venting the smoke through a central chimney on the peaked roofline. Thus the heat produced by cooking was reduced—a result especially desirable during the summer, when separate kitchen buildings also alleviated the humidity of the sultry Tidewater climate. These adaptations were widely adopted in nearby Maryland and throughout the Chesapeake Bay area.

South of Virginia were three very different colonies: the Carolinas and Georgia. Much of what became North Carolina was settled by restless Virginians moving overland, Quakers, and French Huguenots seeking freedom from persecution in their home countries, and Scots-Irish and Germans in quest of cheap land.

South Carolina was more accessible by sea, and it attracted wealthy English colonists who established large rice plantations along the coast and built the port city of Charleston, which became a lively social center. The English philanthropist James Oglethorpe brought the first colonists to Georgia in 1733—many of them people who had faced debtors' prison or suffered from poverty for various reasons, including social class and lack of property. It was an experiment in idealism established with the city of Savannah, a town of broad streets and beautiful squares where the importation of rum was prohibited. However, many of Oglethorpe's beneficiaries found themselves ill suited to become small farmers in a hot, unfamiliar climate, and the

colony's growth was slow. In 1752 the British government took it over and sought to prop it up with large financial grants. Nevertheless, Georgia remained problematic, jealous of the wealthier Southern colonies and plagued by persistent and intractable internal dissension.

Maryland, established as a proprietary colony by Lord Baltimore, was unusual in the number of Roman Catholic settlers who emigrated there, many of whom worked as indentured servants to repay the cost of their passage. Like their Protestant neighbors, they aspired to acquire their own small grants of land and become independent farmers, a goal that many achieved. But as the European market for tobacco continued to grow, these Southern colonies underwent a radical change. Tobacco was a labor-intensive crop that took a heavy toll on the soil, and ever-larger plantations sought a steady supply of cheap labor. By 1619 the first Africans reached these shores on a Dutch ship, and the "peculiar institution" of slavery had become established by 1660. Slave traders seized Africans from the coastal regions of their homeland and sold them to Southern and Caribbean planters in great numbers. A precedent was established that would cause ever-deeper rifts between the North and South, as colonists fought a succesful revolution against England for what Thomas Jefferson had described as their God-given "inalienable rights" to "life, liberty, and the pursuit of happiness." As the new nation spread westward, many questioned the congruence of slavery with the ideals so ably set forth in the Constitution of the United States, the unprecedented document that had been ratified as the basis of a national government in 1789.

Meanwhile, other influences were at work to help shape the emergent nation's diversity. Spain had founded St. Augustine, Florida, in 1565 as an outpost to protect its claim to the peninsula and serve its sailing ships. Its first primitive shelters were palmetto-frond huts modeled on those of the native Seminole and surrounded by a wall. These were soon replaced by wooden huts with thatched roofs that had smoke holes instead of chimneys. A hundred years later, the colonial city of Pensacola was founded on the Gulf Coast,

and Spanish influence extended, at least sporadically, as far north as South Carolina. Familiar with adobe construction techniques, the Spanish used bricks of sun-dried mud and improvised shelters from indigenous materials. In Florida, these included a compound called tabby, made from oyster shells, lime, and sand, as well as coquina stone—sedimentary rock formed by dense layers of coquina shells. By the eighteenth century, larger houses and government buildings comprised in-line rooms centered around a shaded patio, as in the mother country. Balconied second stories were supported on projecting wooden joists called *vigas,* as seen also in the Hispanic Southwest, where the indigenous Pueblo style had much in common with the forms and materials of Spain's vernacular architecture.

French claims to the vast Louisiana Territory drained by the Mississippi River were represented in architecture, customs, and culture extending from eastern Canada and the West Indies to the Gulf of Mexico. In 1755 the English conquest of New France sent some thousands of inhabitants of Quebec and Atlantic Canada into exile. Many of these Acadians (called Cajuns) settled in what is now Louisiana, where they built French-colonial-style cottages raised over a stone cellar covered with stucco. Both levels had porchlike galleries on one or more sides to cope with the humid climate of the bayou marshlands. French-speaking Creoles from the West Indies also built this type of dwelling, especially in New Orleans, the multiethnic port at the mouth of the Mississippi. Farther up the Mississippi River Valley, modest French pioneer houses were constructed of heavy upright logs set into the earth, or slotted onto a timber base called a sill. However, the damp climate and periodic flooding made it expedient to raise these cottages on pillars of rot-resistant cypress blocks, or stucco-covered stone. French settlers included fur traders, small farmers, and, eventually, wealthy Creole plantation owners, who built their mansions along the lower Mississippi. Sugar cane and cotton became the principal crops, shipped by water to American and European markets.

With so many strands of culture and ethnic heritage woven together across the continent, it is no wonder that America is unique among the nations of the world. Both adversity and prosperity helped to shape the national character, and a strong sense of patriotism was forged on the anvil of hard-won experience. The chapters that follow highlight many of the people, places, occupations, and pastimes that are identified with our native land and its heritage of freedom.

Above: *The* Alexandria *sails across the Chesapeake Bay toward the United States Naval Academy, which was established in 1845 at Annapolis, Maryland.*

OLD AS THE HILLS *Left*

Names given to these cave dwellings and their surrounding area in northern Arizona's Canyon de Chelly National Monument give clues to the site's rich history. Known as the *Cañon del Muerto*, the Canyon of the Dead, Navajo who lived here were massacred by Spanish soldiers in the winter of 1804–05. Also known as the "Mummy Cave Ruins" for two well-preserved bodies found there in 1880, today's Navajo residents call it simply *Tsé Yaa Kin*, or "the house under the rock."

THE GREAT AND THE GRAND *Overleaf*

Situated on the banks of Lake Superior, Grand Portage National Monument in Grand Marais, Minnesota, was the most profitable fur trading post on the Great Lakes, its French name describing the "great carrying" of furs between the lake and Fort Charlotte, eight arduous miles away. Changing fashions and diminishing beaver populations eventually led to the demise of the trade, and the monument now pays homage to a way of life that helped change the destiny of the continent.

I SAW THREE SHIPS... *Pages 24–25*

Historic ships at Jamestown harbor in Williamsburg, Virginia, bear such names as *Godspeed* and *Discovery*, symbols of the hopes and dreams of the pilgrims who braved the long and dangerous voyage across the Atlantic and its accompanying hardships.

STEEPED IN TRADITION

Waitresses at Colonial Williamsburg's Shields Tavern, below, offer eighteenth-century hospitality to its clientele. The tavern is part of the 173-acre Historic Area that re-creates colonial life in Williamsburg, Virginia, the capital of the British colony from 1699 to 1780. After meticulous research into all aspects of the preparation and serving of food during the colonial era, everything in the tavern, from the costumes to the place settings and recipes, follows authentically eighteenth-century methods and styles. On the opposite page, a candle-making demonstration bears witness to simpler times at Dearborn's Greenfield Village, Michigan.

ESSENTIAL SKILLS

The colonial way of life is preserved and re-enacted at Greenfield Village, in Dearborn, Michigan. Opposite, "Anna Daggett" dyes wool as her real-life counterpart would have done 350 years ago. Shorthorn oxen, above, are pressed into service to plow a field.

BIENVENIDAS!

Traditional Mexican holiday figures greet visitors to the Riverside, California, Mission Inn, one of the nation's most famous deluxe hotels. Since its development early in the twentieth century by collector Frank Miller, the hotel has witnessed the nuptials of such famous couples as Bette Davis and Humphrey Bogart and Richard and Pat Nixon, who were married here, and the Reagans, who chose the romantic location for their honeymoon.

FELIZ NAVIDAD!

Nuestra Señora Del Espíritu Santo de Zuñiga Mission (below), first established in 1722, was named for New Spain's viceroy Baltásar de Zuñiga. The mission is one of the oldest in Texas. Preservation work began during President Franklin D. Roosevelt's New Deal (1933–41), and the mission is now part of Goliad State Park. A fiesta of fairy lights traces the stonework of San Antonio's San Fernando Cathedral (opposite), the state's first parish church. A marble sarcophagus within contains remains that some historians suggest are those of men who died defending the Alamo in 1836.

PUPPY LOVE

A little boy plays with his puppy at Taos Pueblo, New Mexico. Founded more than a thousand years ago, it is the oldest continuously inhabited community in the nation. So enthralled were the Spanish explorers who arrived here in the sixteenth century that they thought the pueblo was one of the fabled Golden Cities of Cibola.

WITH THIS FAITH *Pages 36–39*

Places of worship provide a venue for faith communities to gather for prayer and reflection. On pages 36–37, a band of patterned shinglework decorates the belfry of this Standard, Vermont, nine-teenth-century church. On page 38, Frank Lloyd Wright's cele-brated Beth Sholom Synagogue in Elkin's Park, Pennsylvania (1954), was designed in close collaboration with Rabbi Mortimer J. Cohen, who envisioned the building as a "mountain of light" symbolic of Mount Sinai. Ridgefield, Connecticut's, beautiful fieldstone Episcopal Church, St. Stephens (page 39), was partly burned by British troops during the Battle of Ridgefield in April 1777—the only land battle on Connecticut soil during the Revolutionary War.

A STATELY TRIBUTE *Right*

A topsail schooner glides across New York Harbor as part of a parade of tall ships paying tribute to Lady Liberty at her 1986 centennial celebrations. A collaborative project between France and America gave the statue a major makeover for the event, adorn-ing her famous torch with gold leaf.

A LIVING HISTORY *Overleaf*

More than forty authentic and reproduction buildings form Pennsylvania's Old Bedford Village, a project devised in the 1970s to invigorate the area's flagging economy while re-creating pre-colonial frontier life to bring living history to new generations. A working farm and study program at the site demonstrate such tra-ditional crafts as blacksmithing, spinning, and broom making.

A MASSACHUSETTS MASTERPIECE *Opposite*

Henry Hobson Richardson's unique Trinity Church, Boston, is the first full expression of his eponymous Richardsonian Romanesque style. With its polychrome stonework—a combination of pink granite and red Longmeadow sandstone—and lantern-shaped tower, derived from the design of the Cathedral of Salamanca, it is one of the city's great treasures.

JAILHOUSE BLUES *Below*

The colonial grandeur and peaceful grounds of Otsego County Jail in Cooperstown, New York, belie its original function as a correctional facility. Today, the historic building houses a state program for preschool children with special needs. The French Second Empire building's elegant mansard roof, characterized by its four concave sloping sides, was a fashionable architectural feature from the 1860s to 1880s.

PAINT YOUR WAGON *Above*

Council Grove, Kansas, was for many years the only trading post on the Sante Fe Trail used by travelers, traders, and freighters transporting goods between Missouri and New Mexico. The wagon pictured here is a remnant of the harsh and hazardous journey made by these frontiersmen and -women.

A SENTINEL IN STONE *Opposite*

Built by the British in 1780 during the Revolutionary War, Fort Mackinac guards the straits of Mackinac Island, on Michigan's Lake Huron. The area's name derives from the Chippewan *Michilimackinac*—"Great Spirit," or "Great Turtle." Originally colonized by French missionaries, the island was taken by the British in 1760. In 1875 part of the island was designated the nation's second National Park, after Yellowstone, and today Mackinac is a magical place whose serenity is maintained by a complete ban on motorized vehicles.

"EQUAL JUSTICE UNDER THE LAW" *Below*

Emblazoned over the doors of the capital's Supreme Court Building, this famous dictum asserts the authority and purpose of the most powerful court in the nation. Sixteen Corinthian columns support the majestic pediment whose frieze celebrates nine figures representing Liberty Enthroned, Order, and Authority.

A SPIRE TO GREATNESS *Opposite*

The 555-foot Washington Monument towers above the city from its vantage-point above the National Mall and at the edge of the Tidal Basin. In springtime, a fabulous floral display is provided by the famous cherry blossoms, donated by the city of Tokyo to the nation's capital in 1912.

TRUTH, JUSTICE, LIBERTY

Above the huge Georgia marble statue that gazes from inside this monument across the reflecting pool toward the nation's Capitol, the following epitaph is inscribed: "In this temple as in the hearts of the people for whom he saved the Union the memory of Abraham Lincoln is enshrined forever." The thirty-six columns represent the number of states in the Union at the time of Lincoln's death.

SOUTHERN BELLES

The live oaks, some 300 years old, lining the approach to Oak Alley (opposite), give the Baton Rouge, Louisiana, plantation house its name and provide an avenue of welcome shade. The hot Southern sun and humid summer conditions inspired landscapers and architects to use every available opportunity to create shade and draw cooling breezes for climate control. Ivy and a high canopy of greenery protect these historic townhouses in Savannah, Georgia (above), from the exhausting summer heat.

SOMETHING OLD, SOMETHING NEW

Below, the nation's oldest city, St. Augustine, takes its name from the saint's day on which Don Pedro Menendez de Aviles, Spain's most celebrated admiral, arrived on the coast of *La Florida*—Land of the Flowers, more than four decades before the arrival of English settlers at Jamestown. The Corinthian and Ionic columns of the New Orleans house on the opposite page typify Greek Revival architecture, while the delicate ironwork lacing the balcony is drawn from the town's rich French culture.

SAIL AWAY *Above*

The seventeenth-century Cape Cod Windmill at Dearborn's Greenfield Village, Michigan, is an example of the many grist mills once found throughout colonial America. This handsome structure still performs its vital function—harnessing the elemental power of the wind to provide kinetic energy for its heavy millstones.

A VIRGINIAN VICTORY *Opposite*

Historic Yorktown, Virginia, is the site of George Washington's victory over the 7,000-strong British army led by Lord Cornwallis in 1781. Now part of the National Park Service's Colonial Parkway, the battlefields are beautifully maintained in memory of what was perhaps one of America's finest hours, while a working farm and living history museum show visitors a glimpse of eighteenth-century daily life and colonial-era warfare.

WAR AND PEACE

These somber scenes commemorate the tumultuous history of Gettysburg National Military Park, Pennsylvania, the site of one of the Civil War's pivotal battles and President Abraham Lincoln's famous address. Above, a row of cannon on Seminary Ridge marks the site of the notorious Pickett's Charge, in which 15,000 Confederate soldiers attempted unsuccessfully to break the Union line. Opposite, the impressive monument to the 4th New York Battery, in Devil's Den, where soldiers from both sides struggled to gain control of this area, with its mass of boulders and rocks that gave the site its name.

A GOLDEN PAST *Previous pages, opposite, and below*

The discovery of "Gregory's Lode" by John Gregory in 1859 heralded the beginning of a virtual stampede to Central City, Colorado (previous pages). Within two months the city's population had swelled to 10,000, and it soon became known as "the richest square mile on earth." Fire destroyed much of the city in 1874, and by 1880 the mines were substantially depleted. On the opposite page, abandoned miners' cabins are seen in fall colors in the scenic surroundings of Telluride, Colorado, where zinc, lead, copper, iron, and silver were mined in addi-

tion to gold, after the first claim was made there in 1875. Today, the town, which is a designated National Historic District, derives its income from its bountiful and ever-replenishing resources of "white gold"—upon which the skiing industry was built. Below, the ghost town of Shaniko, Oregon, was once a thriving community whose own brand of "white gold" was wool: the town was founded as a railroad depot that facilitated the constant traffic of the thousands of bales of fleece generated by the sheep ranches of eastern Oregon.

ANCHORS AWEIGH

The fall season finds Sturgeon Bay, Wisconsin (right), awash with golden sunshine. This idyllic scene belies the early history of Door County, whose name refers to the dangerous waters once nicknamed Death's Door Passage, between the peninsula and Washington Island. Overleaf, a huge sea stack stands proudly alongside one of the 150 shipwrecks claimed by the hazardous shores and tumultuous seas of Washington's Cape Flattery, the extreme northwest point of the Lower Forty-eight states. On pages 68–69, a tractor tug approaches the bow of the ship *Admiral Wm. M. Callaghan* in San Francisco Bay. Rear Admiral William Callaghan was awarded the Legion of Merit for his services directing the Pacific Fleet during World War II and was famed for both his courage and compassion, having insisted upon the burial at sea of a Kamikaze pilot who had died in an attempt to sink Callaghan's ship, the *U.S.S. Missouri*.

A TESTAMENT IN STONE *Page 70*

Salt Lake City's sacred Mormon Temple, completed in 1893, took forty years to build: it is constructed of huge granite blocks hauled individually by ox and wagon from Little Cottonwood Canyon, some twenty miles away from the Utah capital.

MY KIND OF TOWN *Page 71*

When Frank Sinatra sang the line "Chicago is the Wrigley Building," his audience would have been sure to agree—the skyscraper is among the earliest and most famous in the nation. Its architecture combines classical and modern elements: the clock tower is modeled on Seville Cathedral's Giralda Tower, while the building's central plaza allows plenty of natural light to illuminate its interior.

"GIVE ME YOUR TIRED, YOUR POOR, YOUR HUDDLED MASSES..." *Right*

The world's most famous lighthouse stands on the former site of Fort Wood, which protected the New York Harbor, lifting her torch "beside the golden door." Presented to the nation by the people of France, the magnificent 150-foot statue was created by the same engineer as Paris's famous Eiffel Tower.

"THE NEAREST THING TO HEAVEN" *Opposite*

Cary Grant's famous joke in 1957's *An Affair to Remember* captures perfectly the spirit of romance and wonder surrounding New York City's Empire State Building. The movie inspired *Sleepless in Seattle*, whose climactic scene was filmed atop the tower, where the buildup of static electricity can cause sparks to fly from the lips of kissing lovers and St. Elmo's fire to dance from visitors' fingertips.

MEET ME IN ST. LOUIS *Overleaf*

The 630-foot stainless steel Gateway Arch rises from the banks of the Mississippi, forming the centerpiece of the Jefferson National Expansion Memorial Park, which was established in 1935 to commemorate the nation's westward growth in the nineteenth century. Eero Saarinen won the competition to design the monument, which is America's tallest.

NO PLACE LIKE HOMER *Pages 76–77*

The snow-capped peaks of Kenai National Park tower over the Homer Spit, a four-and-a-half-mile natural jetty in Kachemak Bay, Alaska. The small community of Homer swells considerably during the summer months, as thousands of visitors enjoy the area's spectacular scenery and diverse wildlife.

"THE MORNING FOG MAY CHILL THE AIR" *Page 78*

San Francisco's Golden Gate Bridge rises majestically from the famous fog, its towers soaring 750 feet above the city. A masterpiece of civil engineering, the bridge is supported by the huge cables at top, three feet in diameter and constructed of over 27,000 feet of pencil-thick wire.

ONE IN A MILLION   *Page 79*

More than a million vehicles per week cross New York's double-decker, fourteen-lane George Washington Suspension Bridge, making it one of the world's busiest.

CHICAGO, CHICAGO...   *Previous pages*

Grant Park, also known fondly as the city's "front yard," is one of the finest examples of Beaux-Arts landscaping. Its central feature is the Clarence Buckingham Memorial Fountain, donated to the city in 1927 in honor of her brother by the philanthropist Kate Sturges Buckingham. Modeled on the Latona Basin Fountain in Versailles, France, the Georgia pink marble structure is the largest illuminated fountain in the world.

THE GIBRALTAR OF THE PACIFIC   *Left*

Morro Rock, the 576-foot peak that towers above the entrance to California's Morro Bay, is a landmark that has attracted the attention of visitors over several centuries. The last of a chain of long-extinct volcanoes known as the Nine Sisters, the 50-acre feature was named by Spanish explorer Juan Rodriguez Cabrillo on his epic voyage of discovery in 1542.

A LONE-STAR STATE OF MIND   *Overleaf*

The mirrored towers of Dallas, Texas, designed to protect against the sun's intense glare, provide a free lightshow as night draws in. Reunion Tower's distinctive globe, with its patterned illuminations, glistens above the city like a giant mirrorball.

A BRIDGE ACROSS FOREVER   *Pages 86–87*

The Fred Hartman Bridge is the largest cable-staved suspension bridge in the world. Constructed of more than 40 million pounds of steel, the eight-lane, $100-million structure spans 2,475 feet across the Houston ship channel, linking Baytown and La Porte, Texas, near the historic site of the Battle of San Jacinto.

SLEEPLESS IN SEATTLE   *Pages 88–89*

Seattle's elegant skyline gleams above Elliott Bay in the golden glow of the setting sun.

RURAL SCENES
AND FOLKWAYS

Many relics of our colonial and pioneering history have been rummaged from the lofts of old barns, the attics of early houses, dairy cellars, antique trunks, and weather-worn toolsheds. These objects include household utensils, furniture, weathervanes, candlesticks, and farm implements, some of which have been preserved, while others have vanished into the past. Fortunately, the nineteenth century brought a renewal of interest in early American history and a wide range of inventions that made it possible to record folkways and customs as they continued to unfold—including photography, telegraphy, new printing presses, and lithography, among others. And since most of our people came from other lands, or left their original homes here to settle new regions, almost every family brought some of its vital possessions in the form of family Bibles, vegetable and flower seeds, building styles, rifles, tools, and methods of agriculture, which were, in turn, shared with new friends and neighbors. Community spirit resembled that of an extended family, since neighbors depended upon one another for everything from framing up a barn to harvesting crops before they could be destroyed by a sudden storm.

Worship, too, was a communal activity, and countless rural communities centered upon a church or meetinghouse like those we still identify with the New England town green, or the solitary Gothic-style frame church, usually built by its congregation, in the rolling fields of the Midwest. To this day, faith communities of every kind meet regularly for prayer and meditation, putting their spirituality into action by reaching out to others in need. Our original Judeo-Christian heritage has been enriched by religions and philosophies from every part of the world, whose adherents come together in temples, synagogues, ashrams, meditation gardens, private homes—wherever the spirit moves them to gather.

As a result, religious tolerance has grown over the centuries, making our country an example of spiritual as well as material prosperity. Each person is free to worship the Higher Power of his or her understanding, or to refrain from worshipping.

As part of our rural heritage, examples of our houses of worship stand side by side with historic log and clapboard barns, granaries, old farmhouses, one-room schools, and the modest railway stations, often called "whistle-stops," that appeared in the landscape during the nineteenth century. In the Southwest and the Mississippi Valley, French and Spanish missions, respectively, were established to convert Native Americans to Christianity. While

Opposite: This Russian Orthodox church in Karluk, on Alaska's Kodiak Island, is a reminder of the area's Russian heritage.

Below: The shrine at San Antonio's Alamo, Texas, site of the famous 1836 Battle of the Alamo, in which a band of 189 Texans, including such legendary figures as Davy Crockett and William Travis, rebelled against Mexican rule.

the Spanish conquistadors and many wealthy owners of French land grants in the New World have been justifiably denounced for their abuses of power, the great majority of missionaries who accompanied them were sincere. Both members of the Society of Jesus (called the Jesuits) and friars of the Franciscan Order ministered to the native peoples in a spirit of charity, even at the risk of their lives. Many suffered great hardships, including torture and martyrdom, to follow their vocations; this was also true of the many dedicated women of religious orders who came to the future United States to nurse, teach, and otherwise support both native peoples and other immigrants in need.

The Southwest is dotted with adobe chapels and churches like San Francisco de Asis (1710), in Rancho de Taos, New Mexico, and the Chapel of San Miguel (c. 1640) in Santa Fe. Most of the Pueblo-style missions still standing are rugged constructions of timber and adobe encircled by thick walls. Spanish-style landmarks in Texas include the masonry church of San Francisco de Espada (1731) in San Antonio, with its triple bell tower, and a building writ large in American history—the Alamo (1716). It was originally the mission church of San Antonio de Valero, which was secularized long before it became the scene of

battle between American and Mexican forces in 1836. A chain of twenty-one missions, each a day's walk from the other, was founded by the Franciscan Junipero Serra in California. They were lonely outposts for generations, until some of California's major cities began to grow up around them. To this day, the Spanish Colonial style is identified with both California and Florida. The fortresslike appearance of many of their buildings evolved from the Spanish *presidio*, or fort, which served to protect outposts like St. Augustine from attack by competing powers, or hostile natives. Today, we can see smaller versions of these buildings all over the nation, built in the Mission Revival style of the early 1900s, complete with red-tiled roofs, patios, and courtyards.

Enclaves with a French accent are primarily the bequest of our Canadian neighbors and are most apparent in the Mississippi Valley, from Lake Superior to New Orleans and the bayou country around it. The fertile Mississippi and its tributaries provided rich farmland and pasturage, and enterprising pioneers carved homesteads from this region and built simple wooden barns with shingled roofs and cladding. Bayou dwellers depended heavily on fish and shellfish for their food and often lived on wooden houseboats, or

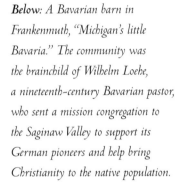

Below: A Bavarian barn in Frankenmuth, "Michigan's little Bavaria." The community was the brainchild of Wilhelm Loehe, a nineteenth-century Bavarian pastor, who sent a mission congregation to the Saginaw Valley to support its German pioneers and help bring Christianity to the native population.

in provincial-style cottages raised above flood level. Farther north, gabled or hipped roofs shed rain and snow, and rain hoods often projected from the peak of barn roofs to protect the hay-mow, where winter fodder was stored, under the eaves. During the nineteenth century, a new wave of settlement swept across the region, and tall windmills brought water to the surface of the Great Plains, which had been inaccurately described by early explorers as "the Great American Desert." On the contrary, both short- and tallgrass prairie (now vanishing rapidly in the wake of overdevelopment) could be worked with newly developed metal plows, which cut through the thick-rooted grasses to the rich, black soil below. The French village of St. Louis, Missouri, soon became known as the gateway to the West, as the "sodbusters" set out to tame the prairie, using the bricklike sod to build their houses and barns and clearing the land of stones for plant-ing, much like their predecessors in New England.

Although the number of family farms in the heartland has now dwindled in the wake of changing demographic patterns, from country to city and suburbs, and of new mechanized methods of agriculture, many working farms in robust health continue to exemplify our rural heritage, from the time-honored Belgian farm

called Heritage Hill in Green Bay, Wisconsin, to the many Amish and Mennonite farmsteads men-tioned in chapter I. In addition, notable historic barns and innovative agricultural complexes have been rebuilt or restored, as seen at Colonial Williamsburg, Virginia; Hancock Shaker Village, Massachusetts; and Shelburne Farms, Vermont. The latter was built as a model farm and agri-cultural estate by William Seward Webb and Lila Vanderbilt Webb in the early 1890s. The origi-nal Breeding Barn was designed by architect Robert H. Robertson and measured more than 400 feet long, 100 feet wide, and two stories high—the largest barn in the United States when it was completed. The Robertson-designed Dairy Barn was used to stable brood mares before it was converted to house a large herd of Jersey cows. The five-story Farm Barn, headquarters for the estate, had a two-acre courtyard and a stor-age capacity of 1,500 tons in the main hayloft. The complex was acquired from the Shelburne Museum in 1994 and is being developed by Shelburne Farms as an independent, nonprofit educational organization. Here, and at numer-ous other facilities, Americans of all ages can learn about traditional methods of animal hus-bandry, crop rotation, hay and grain storage, and diverse styles of vernacular architecture.

Above: An old barn nestles in the rolling hills of Palouse, Washington, one of the nation's most agriculturally productive areas.

93

Farm journals and supply catalogues proliferated after publication of *The American Agriculturist* in 1842, many aimed at specific crops, livestock, and regions. New strains of wheat and other grains became available, along with steam-driven threshers, primitive tractors, and mass-produced metal hardware that replaced hand-forged iron tools, hinges, and ornaments. Now valued as antiques, along with animal-shaped weathervanes and staddle stones that once served as footings for platforms stacked with hay and straw, these artifacts are tangible mementoes of our rural heritage that have become increasingly popular. Another testimony to the vitality of American agriculture and ranching is the continuing interest in 4-H Clubs, county fairs, rodeos, and periodicals like *Country* magazine of Greendale, Wisconsin, with its 250 Field Editors from across the continent, which keeps readers informed about rural America, past and present. Regular features include "Grass Roots Gleanings," "The View from Our Place," "Country Travel," "Great Country Get-togethers," and "Country Churches."

Countless historical societies at the community, state, and national level have documents, early photographs, restorations, and re-creations of our traditional folkways and the occupations they entailed, some of which are almost forgotten. The milking machine has largely replaced the dairymaids who used to work the butter churn, make the cheese, and keep the dairy products cool in a well-scrubbed springhouse. The plowman, with few exceptions, no longer drives a horse or mule to guide the plow along the furrow. Old woodcuts and lithographs preserve such long-time occupations as those of the reaper and the flailer; the gleaner, who picked up cut grain by hand; the corn husker and the corn shocker, who piled the cornstalks into tall shocks; and the many hired hands once needed to bring in the hay, including the loaders, pitchers, and wagon drivers. Automated balers have made the haystack a curiosity, and hay is no longer piled loosely in mows reaching almost to the eaves of the barn.

In *Early America at Work* (A.S. Barnes and Co., 1963), Everett B. Wilson continues the story of

farm workers who have largely passed from the scene, including "the fodderer or fogger, who used to feed the cattle; the crop watcher with his shotgun, as well as that non-human farm hand, the scarecrow, that once used to frighten crows and other birds away from the garden and the corn patch. The limeburner and charcoal maker, who usually were farmers, have all but vanished, as has the bee hunter, who trailed bees to their hives and appropriated their honey. And we never see the bridge owner, a farmer who used to build a bridge—often a covered bridge—over a stream that ran through his property and then charge a toll for its use by others."

Fortunately, we still have some fine examples of those traditional bridges, as well as the water-powered grist mills long used to grind grain into flour, and the self-supporting zigzag fencing that eliminated the need to dig postholes. Maple-sugar houses still bring the sap to a boil in the Vermont countryside, and black-and-white Holstein cows graze beside farm ponds near bright-red dairy barns—the color that has become almost synonymous with our farm architecture. It was introduced by Swedish and German immigrants, who were the first to paint their barns with a mixture of red oxide from the soil, linseed from flax, and casein, from cow's milk. Other farmhouses and barns were whitewashed, using a liquid incorporating powdered chalk. Log barns, with moss or concrete chinking, and slat-sided corncribs, were usually left to weather naturally.

Since timber was so plentiful in early America, the majority of barns, houses, and outbuildings were made of wood, although fieldstone and brick made of local clay were preferred by some settlers, depending upon their availability. Timber-framed barns with board cladding used trees that had been cut down and seasoned for at least a year before they were hand-hewn into squared beams. Framing timbers had projecting tongues, called tenons, and notches (mortises) into which the tenons were pegged securely. At this point, the traditional "barn raising" took place, as neighbors gathered to preassemble whole sections, or "bents," on the ground and raise them on the foundation with long pikes and a derrick. The framing consisted of four or five bents and a horizontal timber called the plate, which connected the tops of the outside posts and supported the rafters. The barn was completed by the addition of siding and roofing—a laborious job in its own right. Accidents were not unknown, as seen by this picturesque epitaph quoted by Eric Sloane in *An Age of Barns* (Dodd, Mead, 1985):

Below: A Washington farmer takes a well-earned rest; the state has approximately 37,000 farms, the majority of which produce such fruit crops as apples—for which the state is famous—and cherries, plums, pears, and blueberries.

John Moody, 1801
Killed at noon on the fourth of November,
In raising his barn he was hit by a timber.
Be ye also ready for in such an hour
cometh the Son of Man.

Certain types of wood were preferred for specific uses. Durable oak was relied upon for framing both barns and houses. Pine, which is weather-resistant, was often used for siding and for ship masts, while rot-resistant cedar served for fencing, tubs, pails, and sills laid on damp ground. Both chestnut bark and pine were favored for shingles, and pliable hickory was readily fashioned into barrel hoops, baskets, and other household utensils. Even masonry buildings like those built by German immigrants to Pennsylvania and other mid-Atlantic regions had wooden armatures to prevent the walls from spreading with changes of temperature. In the coldest parts of the country, masonry barns were seldom used, because frost formed on the inside walls, to the detriment of the animals' health and well-being.

Vertical board siding was the most common cladding on early North American barns; the second most-popular form was horizontal clapboard siding on upright studs. Sometimes narrow strips of wood called battens were nailed along the spaces between the boards to form "board-and-batten" siding for both houses and barns. Not only did this provide better weatherproofing, it made for a neater appearance as well. The "board-and-batten" look is still reprised in many summer resorts and seaside or other vacation homes because of its clean, uncluttered style.

The nineteenth century saw many innovations, including one or more decorative cupolas set along the rooflines of the barn to promote ventilation and the widespread use of silos to store winter fodder above ground. These now-familiar landmarks were built of fieldstone, wood, shingles, and, eventually, metal, and are most apparent on large dairy farms. The advent of widespread sawmills made the construction of new towns and farmsteads much easier and more rapid, and burgeoning transportation systems, including canals, railroads, and roads, linked once-isolated communities more closely and provided the means to ship produce and livestock to urban centers, first in the long-settled East and later in the Midwest and the Far West. Both American and Canadian farmers formed co-operatives and stored their crops in great grain elevators adjacent to the

railroad lines for ready transport to major markets. The once-open range was gradually fenced in, putting an end to the "long drives" of great numbers of cattle to Western railheads and to the range wars between sheep and cattle farmers. Specialization became the norm as ranchers focused on crops like corn and alfalfa for livestock feed; tobacco-growing became concentrated in a few regions; and cereal crops like wheat flourished across huge areas of the Prairie states.

Over time, many of our old barns have been abandoned, to sink back into the earth under the combined onslaught of wind and weather. Fields that had known the heavy tread of oxen and horses, and the whir of birds' wings, have been pre-empted for tract housing, malls, and fast-food restaurants. Fortunately, however, many of our historic barns, farmhouses, outbuildings, and Main Streets have been occupied continuously for generations, restored to fresh vitality, or adapted to new uses that provide an ever-growing appreciation for both our forebears and our contemporaries whose lives have been rooted and centered in the land.

Above: Afternoon sunshine warms this Jackson Valley vineyard. Californian wines are famous the world over, competing fiercely with European growers, whose marketing bosses have, ironically, begun to repackage their wines to mimic the New World style.

MORNING GLORY *Right*

Morning unveils the rolling hills of Washington State's Palouse country and a sheltered farm in Whitman County, between the Rockies and the Cascade Range.

PEACE IN THE VALLEY *Overleaf*

A well-kept ranch in the Methow Valley, near Winthrop, Washington, prepares for winter with secure shelter for its livestock and ample storage for their hay and grain.

UNDER COLORADO SKIES *Right*

A symmetrical red-and-white barn near Granby sports a high-flying kite decoration below the roofpeak and twin wagon wheels beside its entry doors.

TWIN SENTINELS *Page 102*

A towering poplar tree and an old wooden silo bound with metal hoops frame a gambrel-roofed dairy barn in a quiet valley near Monroe, Washington.

THE SUNFLOWER STATE *Pages 103-105*

Kansas wears its agricultural heritage proudly, as seen in an aerial view (page 103) of the checkerboard fields surrounding a farm in Flint Hills. On page 104 is a portion of the Konza Prairie Research Natural Area near Manhattan, Kansas. Page 105 shows a close-up of feathery Indian grass on tallgrass prairieland near Strong City.

A FLOURISHING CROP *Overleaf*

Evening draws down on a weathered corncrib barn surrounded by acres of vigorous young plants in La Salle County, Illinois. Corn is the state's main agricultural product.

SONOMA COUNTY SPRING *Left*

A time-honored California vineyard thrusts its gnarled vines above a sea of mustard flowers; soon, the vines will leaf out and produce the grapes that have made the Golden State's wines world-famous.

A NEW YORK STATE OF MIND *Pages 110 & 111*

We often think of the Empire State as identified with our most populous city, but its 57,000 square miles contain countless long-established farms like these near Syracuse (shown on page 110) and Oswego (page 111).

A GOLDEN PAST *Pages 112-113*

Kent, Connecticut, is the site of this handsome New England-style barn, with its decorative cupola for ventilation and multi-paned livestock windows at ground level. The ample silo is filled with fodder for the coming winter.

ON THE HOOF *Previous pages*

Shorthorn beef cattle find rich pasturage on the plains near Cassaday, Kansas, a prairie state whose fertile grasslands rise gradually from east to west, drained by the Arkansas and Kansas River systems.

FAIRYLIKE BLOSSOMS *Overleaf*

Oregon's Hood River Valley is renowned for its orchards, including the fruit promised by these spring-flowering pear trees near Pine Grove (page 118) and in sight of majestic Mount Hood (page 119).

INCANDESCENT HARBINGERS OF SPRING   *Pages 120-121*

Glowing tulip fields in Washington State's Skagit Valley bear witness to the temperate climate and fertile soil that help make the Northwest famous for its nursery stock and produce.

PACIFIC SANCTUARY   *Pages 122-123*

Hawaii's Hanelei River Valley, on the island of Kauai, with its luxuriant patchwork of tropical flora, is a National Wildlife Refuge as well as fertile agricultural area.

A FISHY BUSINESS   *Opposite*

An experienced fisherwoman arranges her nets on the dock at Kodiak Island, Alaska's third-largest commercial fishing port. The island was the site of Alaska's first non-native settlement, made by Russians from Siberia in the late eighteenth century.

NATURE'S BOUNTY, HUMAN HANDIWORK   *Below*

A cornucopia of California's famous red Zinfandel grapes is poured out by a diligent harvester at Sutter Creek's Aparecio Vineyards.

WHIP CRACK AWAY!

Few other pastimes celebrate the daring and spirit of the all-American male in quite the same way as the rodeo. Such contests as bronco and steer riding, "bulldogging," roping, and tying steers (above and opposite), test the strength, endurance, skill, and courage of their participants to the maximum.

RHYTHMIC COUNTRY REVERIES *Below and opposite*

Alternating circles and squares form a pattern of rare beauty on a weathered barn near Salinas, Michigan (below). On the opposite page, acres of golden pumpkins under a moonlit sky proclaim a banner year for an old Midwestern family farm.

"KEEPSAKE MILL" *Overleaf*

A spring torrent rushes over the weir at War Eagle Mill, with its trim red-and-white buildings, on War Eagle Creek in scenic Benton County, Arkansas.

BACKGROUND EFFECT *Page 131*

Red board-and-batten siding and a white barn window are the ideal backdrop for a stand of broom corn bordered by flowers at Bishop Hill State Historic Site in Illinois.

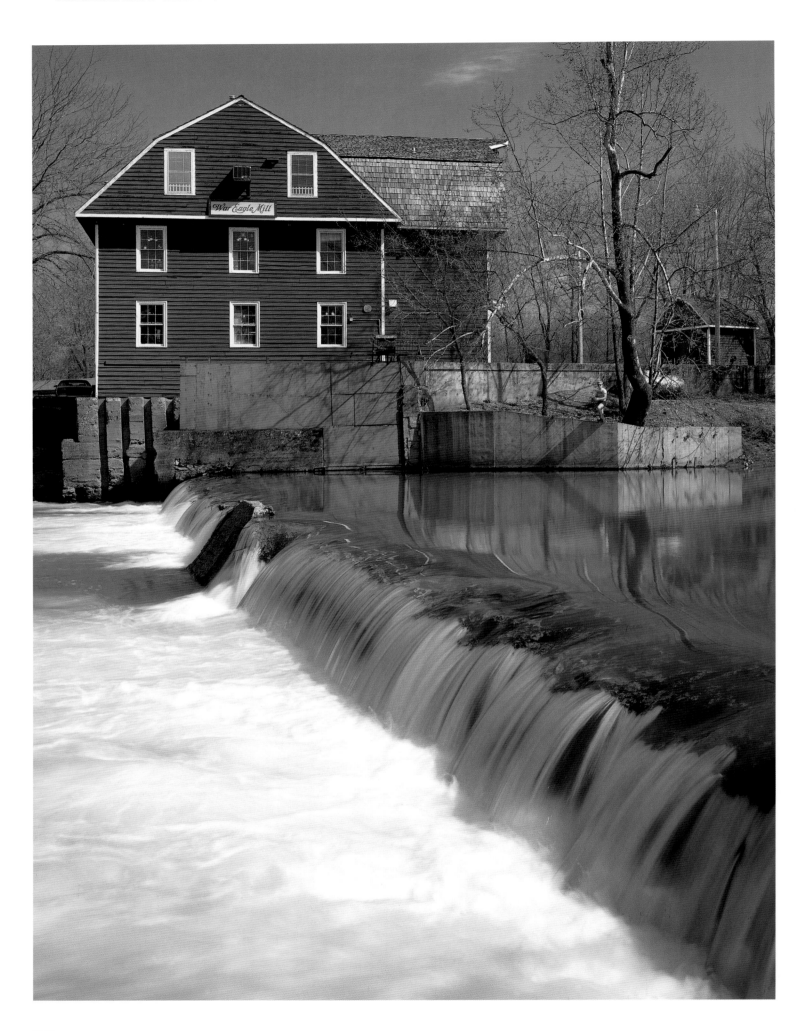

ONLY IN AMERICA *Below and opposite*

A fall scene in Bureau County, Illinois (opposite), combines native prairie grasses, pumpkins, and chrysanthemums with a wagon wheel propped on a split-rail fence. The image below shows a country quilt shop in Intercourse, Pennsylvania, at the heart of Amish country. Handmade Amish quilts in a wealth of traditional patterns are highly desirable collectors' items.

FEED THE WORLD *Below*

A grain truck makes a delivery to St. Anthony, Idaho's, Trost Feed
& Seed Company warehouse and grain elevators for rail transport
to distant markets. Such structures rose alongside Western railways
during the late nineteenth century to provide shipping centers for
farmers on the remote Great Plains of the United States and Canada.

PENNSYLVANIA BARN WITH HEX SIGNS

Albany, Pennsylvania, is the site of this historic "banked barn" (dug into a hillside), with colorful designs painted on the forebay that projects over the livestock quarters. German settlers brought these distinctive motifs from their homeland. Scholars long believed that they were designed to ward off evil forces (from the German word *Hexe*, for witch), but the farmers assert that their function is purely decorative.

PAST INTO PRESENT   *Below and opposite*

Bonneted Amish schoolgirls from Lancaster County look as if they take their studies seriously. The Amish sects have their roots among the Mennonites, who originated in central Europe during the Protestant Reformation. Persecuted for their beliefs, many emigrated to the United States, where they maintain their traditional ways, including the use of horse-and-buggy transport (opposite) and farming with horse-drawn equipment.

MARITIME MEMORIES   *Overleaf*

Maine's seagoing heritage is represented by a small rowboat sheltered in this safe haven at low tide on idyllic Deer Isle, in Hancock County (page 138), and by an array of colorful fishing buoys attached to a weathered building in Rockport (page 139). Timber and commercial fishing have long been mainstays of the Evergreen State's economy, where the annual Lobster Festival has been a top attraction since 1947.

A MASSACHUSETTS HARVEST *Previous pages*

The Bay State's chief crop is cranberries, which grow on trailing bushes rooted in bogs like this one in West Yarmouth. The tart, red berries are harvested in the fall with hand-held scoops on poles. Perhaps they figured alongside the turkey and vegetables in the first Thanksgiving feast, held by the Pilgrims at Plymouth with the help of friendly Algonkian natives.

GOOD TIMES, COUNTRY STYLE *Opposite and below*

The annual Scarecrow Fest in Chappel Hill, Texas (below), draws participants from miles around for home-cooked food, down-home humor, and general camaraderie. A jovial scarecrow—none too scary—is banked by a string of red chili peppers and orange pumpkins to welcome visitors to a roadside stand in Bernadillo, New Mexico (opposite).

FORGING THEIR DESTINY

Of the nation's myriad crafts and traditions, that of the black-smith has perhaps changed the least. The forging and quenching of red hot metal (opposite) is documented in ancient texts. Once the shoes are ready, the horses' hooves are prepared carefully before being shod (above).

GREEN PASTURES *Right*

Sheepherder Jesús Verela and his right-hand dog "Blacky," a border collie, keep a watchful eye on their wooly charges in New Mexico's Carson National Forest.

SKY HIGH *Overleaf*

Towering royal palms soar above a carpet of mustard flowers in Porterville, California, pointing the way to a distant ranch house.

A HOST OF GOLDEN DAFFODILS *Page 149*

This cheerful harvester in the daffodil fields of Washington State's Skagit Valley holds a double armful of fragrant, long-stemmed buds on their way to brighten the marketplace.

THIS
AMERICAN LIFE

When Thomas Jefferson delivered the first U.S. census to President George Washington in 1790, neither of these Founders could have imagined that the new nation's population would grow from some 4 million to more than 250 million before the end of the twentieth century. Thus it is astonishing that our fundamental documents of government, primarily the Declaration of Independence and the U.S. Constitution and Bill of Rights, have withstood the tests of time and monumental social change to build and maintain a free society in a land that is a profile in diversity. As Vincent Wilson, Jr., observes in his introduction to *The Book of Great American Documents* (American History Research Associates, 1998): "The United States of America was the first nation in the world created by the pen as well as the sword; and the ideas expressed in these documents have shaped the lives of all Americans: indeed, these ideas, perhaps more than the vast, rich continent and the American people themselves, have given America its unique identity among the nations of history."

It is not surprising that our past and present capitols are among the most-visited sites in the United States. The nascent government, called the Continental Congress, first met in Philadelphia's Carpenters' Hall in 1774, and the Declaration of Independence was signed in the same city, at Independence Hall, in 1776. Thus the original thirteen colonies, which won the Revolutionary War, became states under the Articles of Confederation, which Congress adopted in 1777 and all the states ratified by 1781.

However, far-seeing statesmen including George Washington, Benjamin Franklin, James Madison, and Alexander Hamilton realized that the new states guarded their individual powers so jealously that the national government would collapse unless Congress took over such essential powers as taxation, the ability to regulate inter-

state and foreign commerce, and the formation of an army. Thus they led a constitutional convention at Independence Hall in the summer of 1787 and drew up the United States Constitution, which was finally ratified by all the states. Meanwhile, other interim seats of government included Congress House in Baltimore, Maryland; the Old Court House in Lancaster, Pennsylvania; the York County Court House in York, Pennsylvania; Nassau Hall in Princeton, New Jersey; and New York City's Federal Hall (1785–90), where George Washington took the oath of office as our first president in 1787.

Not until 1800 did Washington, D.C., the nation's first planned city, become the national capital, designed initially by the French engineer Major Pierre Charles L'Enfant. He advised Congress to "make no little plans" when building the capital, and his advice was followed. Its imposing monuments, created over time by a series of gifted architects and builders, include the U.S. Capitol, with its gleaming white dome rising some 300 feet; the towering Washington Monument, which can be seen from almost everywhere in the city; the majestic Lincoln Memorial, with its sculpture by Daniel Chester French; the Jefferson Memorial, reflected in the waters of the Tidal Basin; and the 132-room White House, the president's official residence, which occupies a beautifully landscaped parklike area at 1600 Pennsylvania Avenue. The original design, begun in 1792, was the work of the Irish-born architect James Hoban, and the mansion was rebuilt and enlarged several times after it was burned by the British during the War of 1812. President and Mrs. John Adams were the first occupants. Other attractions include the original Smithsonian Building, which administers the Smithsonian Institution's world-famous museums and art galleries; the National Archives Building, repository of our documents and records, including the

Opposite: The mining boom town turned ghost town of Rhyolite, Nevada, once boasted three bottle houses like this one, which was built circa 1905 for Tom Kelly.

151

♥ AMERICA'S HEARTLAND

Above: *The main concourse of New York City's magnificent Grand Central Terminal (1903–13). The ceiling mural of a stylized zodiac, the famous clock in the center, and the sweeping marble staircases at either end of the concourse were among the original features that were given a facelift during the restoration of the building in the 1990s.*

Northern states became increasingly industrialized during the war, which created an economic boom that hastened the growth of commerce, industry, and transportation, especially the railroad network that extended nationwide by the late nineteenth century. Railroads were big business, as seen in such imposing stations as New York City's Grand Central Terminal, architect Daniel Burnham's Pennsylvania Station in Pittsburgh, and Philadelphia's Broad Street Station, the work of Frank Furness, a gifted architect who designed more than a hundred depots for the Philadelphia & Reading Railroad during the 1880s. Many of the early Western railways were served by rough-and-ready depots that brought aspiring prospectors to the mining camps of Montana, Nevada, and California, but the powerful West Coast lines, including the Union Pacific and the Santa Fe

Railroads, soon made their mark in the form of stations like the Santa Fe's Casa del Desierto, which included a hotel and restaurant, in Barstow, California, and the Union Pacific's imposing Cheyenne, Wyoming, terminal in the Romanesque style of architect Henry H. Richardson.

African Americans found that they could, in fact, buy land at modest prices through such ordinances as the Homestead Act and cultivate it with good prospects of improving their circumstances. Asian ethnic communities on the West Coast survived decades of overt discrimination to establish enclaves in which they preserved their cultural heritage, worked tirelessly to support their families, and eventually won the respect of their once-grudging neighbors. The Japanese, too, became a presence in the region, working as gardeners, masons, and shopkeepers as well as farmers and holding to their

only to the wealthy, but to the residents of new communities in recently settled regions. Across the nation, Independence Day, the Fourth of July, was—and is—celebrated with fireworks, picnics, patriotic bunting and flags, parades, and decorated bandstands. Rural communities gathered for husking bees, quilting circles, church socials, ice-skating, Bible study, and school sports events. The mining camps were notorious for hard drinking, brawling, brothels, and "claim jumping," but many of the prospectors settled down with the arrival of "mail-order brides" from the East, who had a civilizing influence on their communities. Men who had failed to find gold, silver, or copper turned to other pursuits like farming and mercantile enterprises that prospered them and their regions. Logging, too, was a grueling trade that spawned tall tales told by the lumbermen around their campfires, including the story of Paul Bunyan and Babe, his gigantic blue ox, which have become part of our folklore. Time, tide, and timber built the town of Port Gamble, Washington, under the auspices of New Englanders Andrew Jackson Pope and Frederic Talbot, who founded one of the West Coast's most successful businesses, still in operation after more than a century.

Below: Two favorites of American folklore, Paul Bunyan and his ox, Babe, immortalized by this statue near Crescent City, California.

spiritual heritage of Shinto and Buddhist beliefs and ceremonies. The beauty of their temples and meditation gardens helped to communicate Eastern spirituality to their new country, as did the arrival of Hindu yogis from India, beginning with the revered Paramahansa Yogananda, who came in the early twentieth century, at the instructions of his guru, to found a temple at Mount Washington in Los Angeles and spread the ancient teachings of yoga in the West. The Self-Realization Fellowship that he established soon grew to include many American disciples, one of whom, Sri Daya Mata, came to study at Mount Washington in her teens and has since served the Fellowship, of which she is now president, for seventy years.

Small towns, suburbs, and mountain resorts were served by the ever-expanding railroad network, and leisure activities became available not

155

157

ROCK OF AGES *Previous pages*

The faces of presidents Thomas Jefferson, George Washington, Theodore Roosevelt, and Abraham Lincoln, hewn into the Black Hills of South Dakota, commemorate the founding, growth, preservation, and development of the United States. The Avenue of Flags at the foot of the sculpture is lined with fifty-six standards of the states and territories.

"WHEREVER FLAME MAY RAGE" *Opposite and below*

Santa's sleigh is drawn by a team of Dalmatians at the volunteer fire department of Refugio, Texas. Firehouses across the nation keep these dogs as mascots, a tradition dating from the time of horse-drawn carriages, when the Dalmatian's natural affinity with horses made it an ideal companion to protect travelers and their belongings from highwaymen. The white fire truck opposite, bedecked with strings of brightly colored Christmas lights, blazes a festive trail at Plymouth, California.

AMERICA'S SWEETHEARTS *Previous pages*

A newlywed couple pause for a photo finish, before riding into the Wyoming sunset.

COASTAL CAPERS *Above and opposite*

America's shorelines provide the perfect habitat for both bounteous wildlife and the nation's children, who find endless fascination in combing its beaches and fishing the waters.

SHADY CHARACTERS? *Opposite*

Wearing bright smiles for the camera and dark shades to protect against the sun's glare, this Ugly Dog Competition contestant and its proud owner enjoy the warmth and beauty of a fine summer's day.

THE CELEBRATED JUMPING FROG *Above*

Mark Twain immortalized California's Calaveras County with his short story of intrigue, quail shot, and a jumping frog. A prince among frogs, the winning contestant at the county's Jumping Frog Jubilee, Free Willy, is kissed by three-year-old Cody, his owner and manager, after leaping more than 19 feet over three jumps.

LET'S PLAY BALL! *Opposite and above*

A Little Leaguer in Amador County, California, concentrates before the next play, while second-grade soccer hopefuls in Bellevue, Washington, practice their skills.

AN ALL-AMERICAN PASSION *Left*

The pitcher begins his wind-up at a crucial stage of this night game in the competitive California League. America's favorite sport draws crowds at ball fields large and small, while Major League games attract millions of viewers throughout the world.

BOLD AS BRASS *Opposite and above*

These two images span the spectrum of celebratory styles—the formality of the marching band and the brashness of burlesque. Opposite, the Magic Kingdom's brilliant brass band wows Florida's Disney World crowds. Above, a flamboyant Texan reveler at Houston's Thanksgiving Parade bestows kisses upon her admirers.

"A FLAG APPEARS 'MID THUNDEROUS CHEERS" *Right*

Riders in Fredericksburg's 150th Anniversary celebrations display their Stars and Stripes with pride. German settlers established this Texan town, the last post before the border town of El Paso, in 1886.

HEY MISTER, THROW ME SOMETHING!

The American spirit is at its most flamboyant during New Orleans' Mardi Gras, or "Fat Tuesday." The spectacular carnival dates back to the French tradition of slaughtering a fatted calf (*boeuf gras*) on the last Tuesday (*Mardi*) before Lent. Outrageous costumes (opposite) and house decorations (below) are *de rigueur* during the festival, throughout which revelers catch brightly colored beads and doubloons thrown from the floats.

FLOWER POWER *Overleaf*

Dazzling flowers of fire fill the Texan skies, accompanied by a high-tech laser show, at 1999's Power of Houston Exhibition, which was billed as the "world's largest celebration in the sky"—a fitting welcome to the new millennium. The spectacle covered more than seventy sites over 144 downtown blocks, and more than twelve tons of explosives were ignited during the festivities. The Bayou City, as Houston is known, is itself larger than life, covering 8,778 square miles.

A KODIAK MOMENT

Alaska's Kodiak Islanders celebrate their Russian roots during a performance of this historic play, which features traditional dances and music. First inhabited by the Alutiiq people, the Kodiak Archipelago was colonized by Russians from the mid-1700s and became a major fur-trading hub within a few decades. Fishing has provided the economic mainstay of the island since those years: more than 700 vessels call Kodiak their home port, making this one of America's busiest.

VIVACIDAD!

Vibrant costumes and staccato footwork make this lively Mexican dance an exciting feature of the California State Fair in Sacramento, highlighting the Golden State's proud Hispanic heritage.

DO-SI-DO AND SWING YOUR PARTNER!

Country-style square dancers show us how it's done as they perform at a street fair in North Bend, Washington. Immensely popular, square dancing originated in various traditional dances imported from rural England.

POWWOW *Opposite*

One of approximately 500 dance competitors at the annual powwow of Seattle's Daybreak Star Cultural Center. Hosted by the United Indians of All Tribes Foundation, the celebration attracts more than 10,000 visitors.

EAST MEETS WEST *Below and opposite*

At Houston's Asian Festival (below) and Pearland's Sri Meenakshi Temple (opposite), Texas, the flowing movements of the Thai and Vedic dancers and their ornately patterned costumes, enthrall audiences with their grace and beauty.

SUMMER NIGHTS

An apprentice Hell's Angel streaks the air with a flash of cotton-candy pink (above), while young partygoers in the back of a pickup paint the town red on a hot August night (opposite).

SINGIN' THE BLUES

An impromptu street performance in the French Quarter of New Orleans, birthplace of the African-American jazz style called the blues (short for "blue devils"), with its melancholy tempo and haunting lyrics.

THE FOOD OF LOVE *Below and overleaf*

More than two centuries ago, Thomas Jefferson wrote of his desire for a nation where "music is practiced by every class of men"; he described it as "the favorite passion of my soul." Today, musicians all over America take to the streets, giving us "respite from the cares of the day." Below, a country band warms up behind the Atlas Theatre in Cheyenne, Wyoming. Overleaf, a view from the rear of the stage during a performance in Jacksonville, California.

Don't quit YOUR DAY JOB.

Make it better.

DeVry University Centers.
Undergraduate Degrees.
Post-Bachelor's degree program.
Master's Degrees.
It's all right here.

DeVry offers flexible courses designed specifically for working adults. We're located near where you live or work with classes days, nights, or weekends. So you can earn a degree and improve your day job.

DEVRY UNIVERSITY CENTERS:

Merrillville, IN 219-736-7440
Naperville 630-428-9086
Oak Brook 630-571-1818
Loop 312-372-4900
O'Hare 773-695-1000

OTHER DEVRY UNIVERSITY LOCATIONS:

Chicago 773-929-6550
Addison 630-953-2000
Tinley Park 708-342-3100

www.devry.edu

DeVry University

YOUR BEST CAREER MOVE℠

I'D LIKE INFORMATION ON THE FOLLOWING:

☐ DeVry University Center Bachelor's Degree programs.
(Must be at least 21 years old or have at least 24 hours college credit.)
  ☐ Business Administration
  ☐ Technical Management
  ☐ Computer Information Systems

☐ DeVry University Online Degree programs.
(Must be at least 21 years old or have at least 24 hours college credit.)
  ☐ Undergraduate degrees
  ☐ Graduate degrees

☐ Other DeVry University programs or locations.

☐ DeVry University's Keller Graduate School of Management.

Name _____ Age _____

Address _____

City _____ State _____ Zip _____

Home Phone (___) _____ Work Phone (___) _____ E-mail _____

Highest Degree Completed: ☐ High School   ☐ Associate Degree   ☐ Bachelor's Degree

© 2003 DeVry University. Accredited by the Higher Learning Commission and a member of the North Central Association (NCA), 30 N. LaSalle Street, Chicago, IL. 60602, ncahigherlearningcommission.org

4-3_3V-10M

DeVry University

YOUR BEST CAREER MOVE℠

UP, UP, AND AWAY *Previous pages*

The silence, gentleness, and sheer spectacle of hot-air balloon travel has guaranteed its survival as a popular pastime despite advances in aeronautical technology. Such balloon fiestas as these, in Reno, Nevada, and Albuquerque, New Mexico, paint the skies with glorious color.

PLEASE, MR. POSTMAN *Opposite and below*

All over America, creativity and ingenuity find expression in everyday and unusual places. These mailboxes exemplify America's vibrant folk art—fresh, forthright, and original pieces fashioned by talented amateurs and inspired by local features or characters.

ROOTS AND SHOOTS *Above*

Miwok elders of the California Indian Basketweavers Association gather at Chawse Indian Grinding Rock State Park each month to share their skills with visitors. The ancient craft of fashioning these watertight baskets from reed and raffia developed from a practical need for storage. Intricate and beautiful patterns are created and the baskets adorned with feathers, shells, and other ornaments.

DREAM WEAVER *Below*

The skilled hands of a weaver demonstrate the technique of a much-admired Navajo craft that has been passed down from parents to children for countless generations. The weaving itself is the last in a many-stage process, from shearing the sheep to repeated spinning to dying the wool with natural dyes whose ingredients include juniper, prickly pear, and wild plum. This demonstration takes place at Arizona's Hubbell Trading Post Historic Site, the oldest continuously operating trading post on the Navajo reservation.

BACK IN THE SADDLE AGAIN *Left*

Driving cattle is all about teamwork. Drag riders at the rear of a herd help maintain the pace of a long cattle drive by keeping the slower cows moving. Lead and flank riders steer the cattle from the front and sides, respectively.

BUMPER TO BUMPER *Page 200*

Welded together to withstand the strong winds of the plains in Nebraska, these stacked cars form part of Carhenge. The whimsical full-scale replica of England's megalithic monument was designed and built by sculptor Jim Reinders and his family. Reinders's father once lived on the farmland on which Carhenge stands, and the huge sculpture was created in his memory.

WAGON WHEELS *Page 201*

Another Nebraskan monument to history, this time more locally inspired: two prairie schooners before Scott's Bluff National Monument bear witness to the pioneers who traversed the state during the Westward movement of the nineteenth century.

OUT OF GAS *Pages 202–03*

This lonely gas pump in Garfield County, Utah, has been allowed a well-earned retirement.

LONESOME COWBOYS *Above and opposite*

The world's largest mechanical cowboy, Wendover Will (opposite) stands 90 feet tall, waving visitors across the Nevada state line with a cheerful flash of neon. Named for the resort's founder, William Smith, Will has a younger brother, Vegas Vic, who stands by Las Vegas's famous Fremont Street.

Truxton, Arizona (above), is one waystop on Route 66 where travelers from across the globe can sample some of the area's traditional cooking.

THERE MUST BE AN ANGEL *Above*

Generations of the Delgadillo family have lived and worked in Seligman, Arizona, for decades. Juan, notorious for his practical jokes, runs the Sno Cap Drive-Inn (above). Angel Delgadillo, Juan's brother and President Emeritus of Arizona's Historic Route 66 Society, earned the title of Route 66's Guardian Angel for his efforts in preserving the highway's heritage.

AN IMMACULATE CONCEPTION *Below*

Artist Miloje Milinkovitch takes a well-earned rest after completing his exquisite icon of the Madonna, at the Blessed Virgin Mary Orthodox Church in Fair Oaks, California.

WHEELS ON FIRE *Opposite and above*

The gleaming contours and distinctive snub nose of Nebkota Railway Inc.'s #55 engine (opposite), later acquired by Canadian Pacific Railway. Above, America's classic cars, stars of countless movies, are the stuff of legend. Behind the flaming chassis in the foreground, the hood of another classic car emerges surrealistically from the frontage of this Lakeview, Oregon, car dealership.

ALL ABOARD *Above and opposite*

The California Railroad Museum's Rail Fair provides an opportunity for young and old alike to enjoy a relaxing day out (above). The Cumbres and Toltec Scenic Railroad (opposite) transports passengers from the present day to the age of steam, along the narrow gauge track that links Antolito and Chama near the New Mexico/Colorado border. "I wish that all whose pulse thrills at the sight of Nature's beauties might have been on the train with us that glorious afternoon," enthused a journalist who traversed Toltec Gorge in 1880.

THE SKY'S THE LIMIT *Overleaf*

Michael Hayden's neon sculpture "The Sky's The Limit" sheds a psychedelic glow on Chicago's O'Hare International Airport, named for Lieutenant Commander Edward "Butch" O'Hare. The young fighter pilot's outstanding courage during World War II saved the *U.S.S Lexington*, a mission described by President Franklin D. Roosevelt as "one of the most daring, if not the most daring, single action in the history of combat aviation."

WE ARE THE CHAMPIONS *Left and below*

The American spirit, famed for its competitiveness, creativity, and enormous sense of fun, finds expression in such rural competitions as frying-pan throwing and cherry-pit spitting. The current Guinness World Record distance for spitting a cherry pit is an incredible 95 feet, 9 inches.

FREE THE SPIRIT *Following pages*

On pages 220–21, a photographer prepares to capture these tufts of cloud, racing across the prairies of Rich County, Utah, where high winds sweep across the relatively flat terrain. The county takes its name from the explorer Charles C. Rich, who was commissioned by Brigham Young to find land for Mormon settlements after the 1862 Homestead Act. A torrent of water plummets 620 precipitous feet from the top of the Bridalveil Falls in California's Yosemite National Park (pages 222–23), filling the air with a fine mist, which inspired the Ahwahneechee name for the falls, *Pohono*—"Spirit of the Puffing Wind."

AMERICAN CLASSICS *Opposite and below*

In 1886, the first 25 gallons of a carbonated flavored syrup concocted by pharmacist John Styth Pemberton were shipped in bright red kegs whose distinctive color and inscription now form the world's most widely recognized symbol—as displayed on the wall opposite. The 1903 birthplace of the all-American motorcycle was a 10' by 5' shed in which William Harley, 21, and Arthur Davidson, 20, developed what would become America's Dream Machine, the Harley-Davidson (below).

THIS BEAUTIFUL LAND

The colors and forms of America make a rich tapestry whose threads lead the eye irresistibly from east to west, north to south. On the Atlantic Coast are the ever-changing shades of the sea, from cold granite-gray in the north to the deep blue-green of Biscayne Bay, now an aquatic national park south of Miami, and the waters of the Florida Keys. On their surface, they bear ships of commerce, transport, and pleasure-seeking, and innumerable small craft that ply the waves with wind-powered sails and motors of various kinds. Below the surface, another world offers glimpses of its myriad life forms.

The relative warmth and tranquility of Southern and Pacific waters make them more accessible to both oceanographers and water-sports enthusiasts, including divers and snorkelers. In the Florida Keys, you can watch sand sharks, manta rays, and sleek silver bonefish from flat-bottomed boats. Traveling over these crystalline shallows feels almost like flying. Farther out are the delicate coral caverns of the reefs, alive with jewel-like, multicolored fish, incandescent anemones, and bristling crabs and lobsters, hiding in nooks and crannies to grasp unwary prey.

The warm waters of the Gulf Stream sustain the reefs—composed of trillions of living and dead organisms—and protect them from the ravages of hurricanes and winter storms.

The slow, shallow waters of Everglades National Park, often described as "a sea of grass," are accessible from both the east and west coasts of Florida, with their contorted mangrove trees, roseate spoonbills and other tropical birds, and prehistoric-looking alligators with immense jaws, nearly invisible except for their watchful eyes, which seize any smaller animal luckless enough to pass through their waters, or to drink from nearby banks. The Gulf of Mexico washes the shorelines of states from western Florida to Texas. More than half a million square miles in area, this great curved arm of the Atlantic and its coastal plain is a source of fish and shellfish, minerals, natural gas, and soil enriched by the silt of the Mississippi River and its tributaries, which empty into the Gulf. Historic lighthouses dot these shores, once manned by isolated lightkeepers who doubled as livesavers when a ship went aground, or was battered to pieces by violent storms. Many of these lights now operate electronically; others have been preserved as part of our maritime legacy, serving as museums and landmarks of our long history as a seafaring nation, not only in coastal waters, but in the five Great Lakes that comprise the world's largest freshwater inland sea.

Opposite: The eerie shapes and multicolored layers of sediment in South Dakota's Badlands National Park have been formed by millennia of soil erosion. The area is the world's richest source of Oligocene-epoch fossils, which help trace the evolution of such mammal species as rhinoceros and pig.

Below: The Otter Cliffs, dominating the beautiful coastline of Maine's Acadia National Park, are the highest sheer cliffs on the Eastern Seaboard.

Opposite: A breathtaking view across Bear Lake, in Colorado's Rocky Mountain National Park. Longs Peak is the park's highest at over 14,000 feet.

Below: The beacon at Minnesota's Split Rock Lighthouse State Park was decommissioned in 1969, having cast its twenty-two-mile beam across the deep waters of Lake Superior for fifty years. Each year, the lighthouse is lit to commemorate the 1975 sinking of the freighter SS Edmund Fitzgerald, with its crew of twenty-nine men.

On the Pacific Coast, tall forests of yellow-brown kelp, anchored to the ocean floor by holdfasts, provide food and shelter for countless creatures. Tiny mollusks and worms cling to their hundred-foot stalks, and lean barracudas swim among them in search of prey. Sea lions dive deeply off the coast of the Golden State, and sea otters, once hunted almost to extinction, sleep and play in the tangled mat of kelp fronds on the surface. California's Channel Islands—the tips of an ancient mountain range—are wreathed in wildflowers in the spring and filled with colorful tidal pools and seabirds all year round. December brings the gray whale for a stopover in the kelp feeding grounds on its 5,000-mile migration from the Arctic to Baja California.

Sea stacks and arches carved by the waves from islands of stone lie just off the coast of Oregon and Washington State, where beachcombers can roam for miles exploring the shoreline. Portland, Oregon's, profuse rose gardens recall the New England region from which many of its settlers

came to make a new life along the majestic Columbia River, the largest in the West. Snow-crowned Mount Hood is the city's pride, as glacier-clad Mount Rainier is a symbol of Seattle and the heart of a national park comprising almost 250,000 square miles. These and other peaks of the Cascade Range help account for the temperate climate on the ocean side of our "Lower 48" Northwestern states, where rainfall is abundant; on the other side of the mountains, a much drier climate prevails. Oregon's Crater Lake, the nation's deepest, is a sapphire set in the crown of Mount Mazama, a volcano that erupted more than 7,000 years ago. It, too, is the centerpiece of a national park that preserves its pristine wilderness setting.

Three worlds in one converge in Washington State's Olympic National Park, whose features include the restless seacoast, luxuriant rainforests, and the regal Olympic Mountains. The ragged sea stacks offshore were once part of the mainland—headlands that jutted into the ocean and were gradually eaten away by the relentless surf.

Above: Altamont Pass is one of three Californian wind farms supplying nearly a third of the world's wind-generated electricity. Together, they harness enough power to supply a city the size of San Francisco.

Now seabirds nest on these rocky islets, safe from landbound predators. Beyond the shoreline, forests stretch toward the interior of the Olympic Peninsula. In four ocean-facing river valleys, moderate temperatures and very high annual rainfall (140 inches) combine with heavy fog to create a botanical paradise: the Olympic rainforest, finest remnant of the once extensive Northwestern rainforests. Here broadleaf black cottonwoods and arching vine maples are festooned with curtains of greenery that filter the sunlight onto the forest floor, sown thickly with ferns and rare wildflowers. Roosevelt elk, snowshoe hare, and Douglas squirrels make their homes here. Then the land rises abruptly toward the subalpine meadows of the Olympics, whose highest slopes may receive more than 30 feet of snowfall per year. Glaciers mantle these peaks, where the winter's long silence is broken only by hissing gales and the occasional dull boom of an avalanche.

Several decades ago, almost 44 million acres of Alaskan land became part of the National Park System, when seven new reserves were created on the nation's last frontier. At Glacier Bay, one can see the land as it must have looked at the end of the last Ice Age. The jagged coast, with its count-less inlets, bays, and fjords, is longer than that of all the lower forty-eight states combined. Katmai National Park, on the Alaskan Peninsula, and Kenai Fjords, on the Gulf of Alaska, also preserve the coastline. The wilderness parks of the interior range from Gates of the Arctic to Wrangell-St. Elias, the largest area—more than 8 million acres—administered by the National Park System.

By way of contrast, the last of the Pacific states, Hawaii, is an archipelago of subtropical islands in the North Pacific, more than 2,000 miles south-west of San Francisco. The islands are the tips of ancient volcanoes, several sparsely inhabited, others, including Hawaii itself, called the Big Island, among the world's most-desired resorts, with beaches formed of black lava sand and jungle-covered peaks alive with tropical birds and brilliant flowers. The Big Island has two of the world's most active volcanoes—Kilauea and Mauna Loa—which shoot fire-fountains of lava hundreds of feet into the air. Lava also flows from vents in the mountainsides, obliterating everything in its path. Once the flow has cooled, however, favorable rain-bearing trade winds soon clothe the slopes in tiny algae and lichens, then in emerald colonies of moss and fern. In time, a new forest will spring up here.

The contours of the American mainland are as diverse as those of its surrounding seas. Northern New England still has many areas that are heavily forested, and rugged outcroppings of stone attest to the passage of Ice-Age glaciers throughout the region. Early farmers here built the sturdy rock walls that marked their boundaries from the stones they dug up from their grudging fields. Southern New England is more densely populated, with many historic towns centered on the village green with its white-steepled Congregational church, and the centuries'-old cities of Boston, Hartford, and Providence. The nation's first public schools evolved here, as well as most of our early institutions of higher learning.

Among the other original thirteen colonies are the mid-Atlantic states, ranging from the scenic Catskill and Adirondack Mountains of "Upstate" New York to the rich, rolling fields of Pennsylvania and New Jersey, which combine a long history of productive farming with more recent developments in industry, technology, and transportation. The Delaware River has been a major artery here since colonial days, and it still waters a region of rushing streams that once powered grist mills and still attracts fishermen in search of speckled trout, bass,

and the legendary "one that got away." Among the area's major attractions is Philadelphia's National Historic Park, a veritable treasure trove of American history and architecture.

The climate grows warmer as one moves south into the Tidewater area, where the shining expanse of the Chesapeake Bay plays a major role in the region's life and commerce. The nation's capital hums with political, cultural, and international events, providing the venue for democracy in action with stirring protests, rallies, marches, and lobbying for every conceivable cause. Other cities of major historic interest—Charleston, Savannah, Atlanta, Mobile, and New Orleans, among others—star the coastal plain, interspersed with large tracts of rolling hills and highlands farther inland. The Southeast has an amazing variety of natural attractions, from Kentucky's bluegrass country, where graceful thoroughbreds are groomed for the racing circuit, to the breathtaking Blue Ridge and Great Smoky Mountains. At Hot Springs National Park, Arkansas—which features forty-seven hot springs of reputed medicinal value—wild turkeys roam the wooded hillsides around the famous health spa, and black bears have made a comeback.

Below: Wyoming's Yellowstone National Park, the only location in the Lower Forty-eight states where a population of wild bison has existed since prehistoric times. Winter finds the herds congregating around the Upper Geyser Basin and other geothermal areas, where snow melts quickly on the warm soil.

From Missouri northward, the coastal plains shade into the central plains, with the isolated Ozark-Ouachita Highlands rising higher than any land between the Appalachians and the Rocky Mountains. The Midwest, long considered to be America's heartland, is a distinctive region settled by many immigrants from Germany, Scandinavia, and Eastern Europe who cultivated the land, built railroads and stockyards, and were instrumental in founding such strong, prosperous cities as Chicago, Minneapolis, Columbus, Indianapolis, and St. Louis. The Ohio and Mississippi Rivers, with their tributaries, as well as the Great Lakes, are the principal waterways of this landlocked region, whose people take pride in their steady contribution to the American scene, both rural and urban.

Farther west, the diverse Mountains and Plains regions offer some of the most impressive scenery in the continent: Kansas's tall-grass prairies, Nebraska's Chimney Rock, the Dakota Badlands, northern Montana's beautiful Glacier National Park, Wyoming's Grand Tetons, Utah's intricate, multicolored Bryce Canyon National Park—one of seven in the state—and the grandeur of the Colorado Rockies. Here it is still possible to see the land as it was before human eyes looked upon its fantastic rock formations; plunging ravines; high, arid plateaus; and inaccessible snow-crowned heights. Yellowstone National Park—the world's first (1872)—is a huge area of unspoiled wilderness spanning parts of three states: Wyoming, Montana, and Idaho. Some 10,000 geysers and hot springs erupt from far below the surface here, and moose and elk range widely. Obsidian cliffs, petrified trees, lodgepole pines crowding to the banks of the Yellowstone River...all this led the passionate novelist Thomas Wolfe to write: "It is a fabulous country: the only fabulous country."

From the Rockies, the Colorado River rushes toward the arid Southwest, carving out the mile-deep Grand Canyon. The dizzying view across its widest expanse, shimmering with shades of red, pink, copper, gold, and orange that change with the light of day, is indeed one of the wonders of the world. But the Southwest has many other beauties, from blazing, seemingly lifeless deserts that are, in fact, teeming with hidden creatures of the night and rugged plant forms to the vast reef of the Guadalupe Mountains, once undersea, which tower suddenly from the yucca-studded flatlands of Texas. The Lone Star State's Big Bend National Park bristles with spiny thickets of lechuguilla that shelter pronghorn antelope and mule deer and provide forage for bands of tough-skinned collared peccary. These wild pigs, called javalina, also thrive on the desert's prickly pear and the beans of the mesquite, whose root system can reach 100 feet into the earth in search of moisture.

In northeastern Arizona, the Painted Desert unfolds in a panorama of banded dunes and patchy grasslands rainbowed in shades of rust, slate blue, topaz, tobacco, and amethyst. In this region is Petrified Forest National Park, where trees that fell some 200 million years ago were carried by turbulent rivers to the lowlands when giant reptiles and amphibians dwelt here. These ancient ancestors of the Norfolk Pine were covered deeply in mud, sand, and volcanic ash. Minerals like silica gradually penetrated the wood and crystallized in the form of quartz. In time, the trees were turned to stone. Here they remained until some 65 million years ago, when the Southwest was wracked by the slow geologic convulsions that uplifted the Rocky Mountains, the Colorado Plateau, and the long-buried floodplain where the fossil trees had been entombed. Thousands of other fossils are found here too—delicate stone tracings of long-vanished leaves, cones, fern fronds, mollusks, and fish that flourished here millennia ago.

Rich earth colors of every hue and clear, cloudless blue skies have made the Southwest a mecca for artists and artisans, who flourish in Taos, Santa Fe, San Antonio, and many other communities. They include painters and sculptors, pottery makers, weavers, silversmiths, architects, landscape designers—some who originated here, including notable Native American artists, and others who were attracted by the region's unique multicultural heritage and scenic beauty. It is gratifying to see more and more visitors from around the world coming here and to other parts of our country to experience the many sights, sounds, tastes, customs, landmarks, and most of all, people, that make up the land we call home.

SUNSET ON SHENANDOAH *Previous pages*

The establishment of Virginia's Shenandoah National Park by President Franklin D. Roosevelt in 1926 created a pastoral retreat in the Blue Ridge Mountains, close to the nation's capital. The beauty of the bluish haze, from which the range takes its name, is most pronounced at sunset.

CLIMB EV'RY MOUNTAIN *Opposite, above and overleaf*

Mirrored in the stillness of the lake, the twin peaks of the Maroon Bells (opposite) in Colorado's Snowmass Wilderness, near Aspen, are possibly the most photographed in the world. At over 20,000 feet, Denali (above, formerly known as Mount McKinley) is the highest peak in the United States. The Athabascan name means "The High One." A colorful carpet of alpine wildflowers, including lupine, valerian, and paintbrush, emblazons the meadows at the foot of the Mazama Ridge, in Washington's Mount Rainier National Park (overleaf).

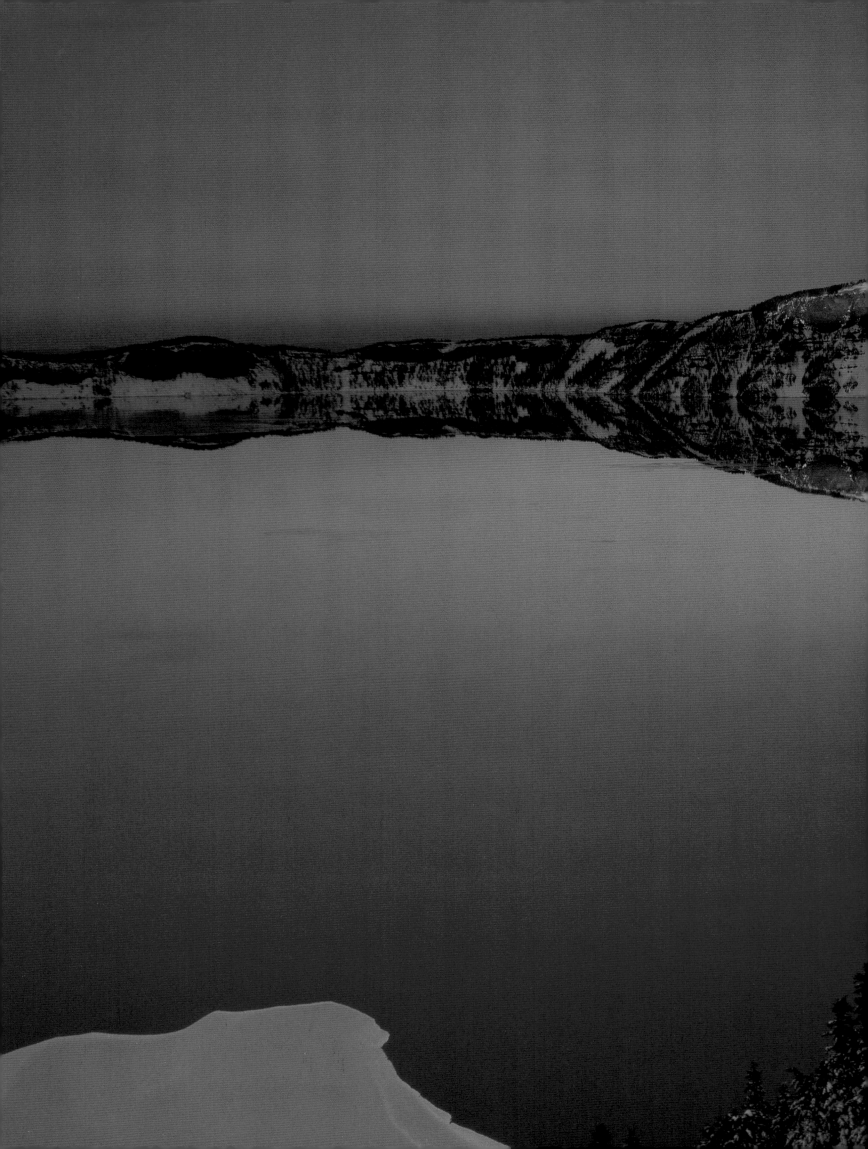

OUT OF THE DEPTHS *Previous pages*

At nearly 2,000 feet deep, Crater Lake is the nation's deepest. The crater was formed by the collapse of a vast volcano some 7,700 years ago during an eruption forty-two times more powerful than that of Mount St. Helens in 1980. The 4.6 trillion gallons of collected snowmelt and rainfall are both protected and sealed off by the steep rim, giving the water an extraordinary clarity and stillness.

A VISION IN THE MIST *Pages 242–43*

According to legend, St. Mary Lake, deep in the heart of Montana's Glacier National Park, was named by the Belgian Missionary Father Pierre Jean DeSmet, who, stranded one morning in thick fog, saw the saint's face on the sheer slope of Divide Mountain as the mist cleared.

THE MAGNIFICENT TETONS *Pages 244–45*

Wyoming's Grand Teton National Park is one of the nation's most unspoiled territories. The long-abandoned Pfeiffer's Homestead, in the foreground of this photograph, now sees little activity apart from the wildlife roaming the sagebrush flats.

IN THE BLEAK MIDWINTER *Above and opposite*

Pine needles spangled with hoar frost frame the sheer granite face of Yosemite's Half Dome (above), an 8,842-foot giant looming far above the valley. The mountain's "other half" was split away when the glaciers receded after the last Ice Age. The 7,600 foot Liberty Bell, opposite, is one of the most rugged peaks in Washington's Cascade Mountain Range.

WHERE BUFFALO ROAM *Pages 246–47*

The Hayden Valley, irrigated by the Yellowstone River in the national park of the same name, is a feeding area for bison, a species that was almost extinct a century ago, but is no longer endangered.

OLD MAN RIVER   *Page 248*

The 500-foot bluff overlooking the Mississippi River at Pike's Peak, Iowa, takes its name from the famous eighteenth-century explorer Zebulon Montgomery Pike, who led an 1805 expedition to explore the area. The beautiful scenery, with its rolling hills, slow-moving river, and deep, lush valley, is characteristic of the "Driftless Region," a large geographical area that escaped the leveling effect of Ice-age glaciers.

PICTURE THIS!   *Page 249*

The Pictured Rocks on the Michigan shores of Lake Superior take their name from the images created by mineral deposits on the cliffs. The Miner's Castle is perhaps the most striking of the spectacular rock formations along the lakeside.

THE "GREATEST MEETING OF LAND, SEA, AND SKY"   *Left and overleaf*

California's Monterey County boasts, in Big Sur, one of the world's most spectacular coastlines, described by novelist Henry Miller as "a region where one is always conscious of eloquent silence…the face of the earth as the Creator intended it to look." The photograph overleaf features a waterfall at McWay Creek, Julia Pfeiffer Burns State Park. Vivid purple Pride of Madeira flower heads enliven the headlands above the coast, shown at left.

HAWAIIAN PARADISE   *Pages 254–55*

Palm and Hala trees border Waikoko Bay (page 254), while the black boulders on Lumahai Beach (page 255), immortalized in the 1958 movie *South Pacific*, testify to its volcanic origins. Kauai was the first of the major Hawaiian Islands to be free of volcanic activity.

AN OLYMPIC IDYLL   *Pages 256–57*

Silhouetted against a spectacular sunset and reflected in the shallows of Shi-Shi Beach, the Point of Arches headland is one of the highlights of Washington's Olympic National Park.

TRUTH OR DARE *Below*

The serene scenery of Bodie Island, one of the barrier islands on the beautiful Outer Banks of North Carolina, conceals the mysterious history of Dare County. The first child born in the New World to English colonists in 1587, infant Virginia Dare was one the Roanoke Islanders who vanished mysteriously that same year.

TRANSCENDENT BEAUTY *Opposite and overleaf*

The rolling dunes and ocean shores of Cape Cod, Massachusetts, have inspired a host of artists and writers, including the transcendentalist Henry David Thoreau, whose *Cape Cod* eulogized the area's rugged beauty. The lighthouses along these shores, including those at Great Point, Nantucket (opposite), and Nauset Beach (overleaf) have witnessed many changes, not least the Cape's transition from whaling community to popular resort.

GEORGIA ON MY MIND *Right*

The morning sun sheds a golden glow over this deserted beach on Jekyll Island, Georgia, once the ocean playground of such American luminaries as J.P. Morgan, William Rockefeller, Joseph Pulitzer, and Marshall Field. Events that shaped the nation's destiny, including the first transcontinental telephone call and the drafting of the Federal Reserve Act, took place just a few miles from this spot.

ISLAND LIFE *Previous pages*

The golden sands of Padre Island, named for seventeenth-century missionary Padre Jose Nicolas Bali, extend ten miles along the Texas Gulf Coast. Its waters teem with life, feeding five of the world's seven species of sea turtle and the millions of birds alighting from the Central Flyway above.

LADY OF THE LAKE *Overleaf*

The Wisconsin Point Lighthouse in Douglas County provides one of the finest views of Lake Superior, whose name heralds its status as the largest freshwater lake in the world, at 3,200 square miles.

SPRINGING WATERS *Previous pages*

On page 268, water carves a passage through a sheet of columnar basalt in Oregon's Umpqua National Forest. These idyllic falls so delighted the Chinook that they were named *Toketee*—"graceful" or "pretty." A torrent of snowmelt plummets 620 feet from the top of Multnomah Falls in the Columbia Gorge, Oregon (page 269), one of the nation's highest year-round waterfalls. Winter chills can freeze the falls, transforming them into gigantic icicles.

WADERS OF THE WETLANDS *Right*

A large community of egrets competes for space and food in Florida's Everglades National Park, the nation's only subtropical preserve. The park is known not only for the rich birdlife that thrives in the shallow waters and mudflats, but for its sheer diversity of wildlife, including the alligators and crocodiles that lurk here—the only place in the world where they can be found side by side.

A NATURAL CATHEDRAL *Overleaf*

Such streams as this one in Soleduck Valley (page 272) carry the persistent rainwater through the verdant forests of Washington's Olympic National Park. The gigantic broadleaf maples on page 273, cloaked with club mosses, invite comparison to the columns of a vast cathedral, supporting an emerald roof through which shafts of sunlight penetrate the dense rainforest foliage of the park's Hoh River Valley.

SPRINGS ETERNAL *Opposite*

In 1916, drillers on Washoe County's Fly Ranch, Nevada, struck geothermal water, creating the Fly Geyser, a drill well that acts as a natural spouter. Over the years, deposits of travertine have created terraces around the geyser.

THE ANCIENT ONES *Below*

The White Mountains of Inyo National Forest, California, are home to the world's oldest living inhabitant, the Bristlecone pine. Inhospitable conditions provide an environment in which the trees have become so hardy that they survive the harshest elements and the passage of time—the oldest, Methuselah, is nearly 5,000 years old.

AN UNEARTHLY LANDSCAPE *Following pages*

Yellowstone National Park is home to more than 500 geysers, a greater concentration than any other place on Earth. The Great Fountain (pages 276–77) erupts twice, sometimes three times a day, shooting a column of water up to 250 feet into the sky from a podium of terraced reflecting pools. On pages 278–79, winter steam and melted snow betray the presence of thermal activity.

CANYON COUNTRY *Previous pages, below, and opposite*

The magnificent hoodoos and pinnacles of Agua Canyon (previous pages) in Utah's Bryce Canyon National Park bear such imaginative names as Hunter and Rabbit. These extraordinary pillars of gnarled and ridged rock, formed by erosion over millions of years, continue to crumble into the valley floor. Similarly, the persistent flow of rivers has etched spectacular canyons deep into the bedrock at Waumei Canyon in Kauai (below) and, most famously, at Arizona's Grand Canyon, opposite, seen here from a vantage point on the South Rim.

DESERT COLORS   *Previous pages*

The hostile heat and parched soil of Arizona's Organ Pipe Cactus National Monument and Ajo Range (pages 284–85) foster an abundance of wildlife adapted to its climate. Its eponymous cactus stores water in its multiple "pipes."

SANDS OF TIME   *Below and opposite*

Ripples of shifting sand at the Mesquite Flats Sand Dunes (opposite) and the strange wakes left by the mysterious sliding of rocks across the Racetrack Playa (below) bear witness to the searing heat of Death Valley, California, the hottest, driest place in North America.

WALKING WITH GIANTS *Page 288*

The Giant Seqouia, the world's tallest tree, is found only on the slopes of eastern California's Sierra Nevada. This specimen in King's Canyon National Park is a neighbor of the General Grant Redwood, which was dedicated as the nation's Christmas tree by the U.S Department of the Interior in 1926.

RIO GRANDEUR *Page 289*

The rugged rock of Mesa de Anguila in Big Bend National Park, Texas, glows with a warm golden hue in the intense sunlight. The Rio Grande's relentless passage has carved a deep ravine, Santa Elena Canyon, through this part of the Chihuahuan Desert.

FIRE AND ICE *Below and opposite*

In the temperate climate of the Northwest, sunshine against the snow brings a brilliance and sharpness of color to winter scenes. Below, a quartet of swans, warmed by layers of down, drifts gently along the Madison River, Wyoming. A Yuletide blanket of virgin snow covers the firs in Montana's Gallatin-Targhee National Forest, opposite.

A DESERT SANCTUARY *Overleaf*

First named Zion by Mormon missionary Isaac Behunin, who was seeking refuge there from religious persecution in 1863, and declared a national monument in 1909, Utah's Zion National Park inspired such awe in its early visitors that many of its features were given Biblical and religious names. The Pulpit (pictured) is surrounded by the Temple of Sinawara, a vast natural amphitheatre ringed by steep cliffs.

SMOKY SPLENDOR   *Pages 294–95*

As winter approaches over the Great Smoky Mountain Range on the North Carolina/Tennessee border, more than 100 species of tree provide a spectacular display of dappled color. The blue mist caressing the mountain peaks inspired the Cherokee name for the area—*shaconage*, or "land of the blue smoke."

FROM ONE, MANY   *Left and previous pages*

The morning sun illuminates golden leaves of aspen in this Gunnison National Forest grove (pages 296–97). In springtime and summer, a canopy of vivid green leaves allows sunlight to filter through to the forest floor in Montana's Red Rock Lakes National Wildlife Refuge (left). The most widely distributed species of tree in North America, encompassing the continent's four corners, is also Earth's largest living organism: although the trees appear to be individual plants, each aspen grove ultimately stems from a single root.

RED, GOLD, AND GREEN *Below and opposite*

The pale light of a spring morning illuminates these trees across from Roark Bluff in Arkansas's Buffalo National River (below). Opposite, sugar maples and yellow birch trees give a fiery display of color during the fall at the mixed hardwood forest of Maine's Acadia National Park.

INDEX

Acadia National Park, ME 225, 225, 300, 301
Adams, John 151
Adirondack Mountains, NY 155, 229
adobe construction 8, 19, 92
Affair to Remember, An 73
Africa, Africans 13, 18 see also slavery
African American, African Americans 154, 188
agriculture 10, 14–19, 29, 90–149 see also ranches, ranching; rural America
Agua Canyon, UT 280–81, 282
airports see individual names
Ajo Range, AZ 284–85, 286
Alamo, the, TX 33, 91, 92: shrine 91, 91, 92
Alaska 7, 10, 73, 91, 124, 180, 228
Alaskan Peninsula 228
Albany, NY 15
Albany, PA 135, 135
Albuquerque, NM 194
Alexandria, The 19
Altamont Pass, CA 228
Amador County, CA 168, 169
American Agriculturalist, The 94
Amish 16–17, 93, 133, 136, 136, 137 see also Mennonites
Annapolis, MD 19
Anne, Queen of Britain 156
Aparecio Vineyards, CA 124, 124
Appalachians, the 7, 153, 230
architecture see individual styles and buildings
Architecture of Country Houses, The 153
Arctic 226
Arizona 21, 197, 207, 208, 230, 282, 286
Arkansas 128, 229, 300
Arkansas River 117
Asians 7, 13
Aspen, CO 235
Atlanta, GA 229
Atlantic 21, 225: coast 7, 14, 17, 153, 225; mainland 7; Mid- 14, 97, 229
Atlas Theatre, WY 189
Austria 156
Avenue of Flags, SD 158–59, 160
Aviles, Don Pedro Menendez de 54
Babe 155, 155
Badlands National Park, SD 224, 225, 230
Baja California 226
Bali, Padre Jose Nicolas 264
Baltimore, MD 151
Baltimore, Lord 18
Bandelier National Monument, NM 13
Baptists 16
Barlowe, Arthur 8
Barnes, A.S. & Co. 94
barns 14, 15, 16, 17, 91, 93, 93, 92–93, 94, 96–97, 102, 106, 106–7, 128, 128, 131: banked 135, 135; Bavarian 92; Breeding Barn, VT 93; clapboard 91, 97; corncrib 96, 106, 108–9; Dairy Barn, VT 93; Dutch Colonial 8, 15; Farm Barn, VT 93; log 8, 91, 96; New England-style 112–13, 117; Pennsylvanian bank 16; tobacco-drying 17; wooden 92, 96, 97
Barns, An Age of 96
Barstow, CA 154
baseball 170–71, 171
Baton Rouge, LA 52, 53
battlefields 56, 59, 83 see also individual names
Bauhaus, the, Germany 156

Bavaria, Germany 92
Bayou City see Houston, TX
bayou country 19, 92–93
Bay State see Massachusetts
Bayton, TX 83
Bear Lake, CO 226, 227
Beaux-Arts landscaping 80–81, 83
Behunin, Isaac 291
Belgium, Belgian 93, 94, 240
Bellevue, WA 169, 169
Benton County, AR 128
Bernadillo, NM 142, 143
Beth Sholom, Synagogue, PA 38, 40
Big Bend National Park, TX 230, 289, 291
Bigfoot 204
Big Island see Hawaii
Big Sur, CA 250–51, 251, 252–53
Bill of Rights, U.S. 151
birds 270, 270–71, 291
Biscayne Bay, FL 225
Bishop Hill State Historic Site, IL 128, 131
bison 229, 229, 240, 246–47
Black Hills, SD 158–59, 160
Blessed Virgin Mary Orthodox Church, CA 209, 209
Blue Ridge Mountains, VA 229, 232–33, 235
boats 8, 10, 21, 24–25, 40, 40–41, 54, 64, 64–65, 68–69, 76–77, 92, 125, 136, 138, 225, 266–67
Bodie Island, NC 258, 258
Bogart, Humphrey 30
Book of Great American Documents, The 151
Boone, Daniel 7
Boston, MA 14, 44, 45, 229
Bridalveil Falls, CA 219, 222–23
bridges 64–65, 79, 83, 86–87: covered 94, 95, 96 see also under individual names
Britain, British 18, 40, 46, 54, 151, 156
Broad Street Station, PA 154
Bryce Canyon National Park, UT 230, 280–81, 282
Buckingham, Kate Sturges 83
Buddhism 155
buffalo 13
Buffalo National River, AR 300, 300
buildings 12–89, 92, 97, 151–57 see also individual names
Bunyan, Paul 155, 155
Bureau County, IL 132, 133
Burnham, Daniel 154, 156
cabins, log 8, 17
Cabrillo, Juan Rodriguez 83
cacti 284–85, 286
Calaveras County, CA 167, 167
California 8, 9, 10, 30, 64, 73, 83, 92, 97, 117, 124, 146, 154, 155, 156, 160, 167, 169, 181, 189, 196, 205, 209, 212, 219, 226, 228, 230, 251, 274, 286, 291: Indian Basketweavers Association 196, 196; League see also baseball 170–71, 171; Railroad Museum's Rail Fair 212, 212; State Fair 181, 181
Callaghan, Admiral Wm. M. 64, 68–69
Callaghan, Rear Admiral William 64
Cambridge, MA 157
camping 9
Canada 9, 16, 17, 19, 92, 97, 134
Canadian Pacific Railway 211
canals 97 see also individual names
Cañon del Muerto 21
canyons 9, 282 see also individual names
Canyon de Chelly National Monument, AZ 20–21, 21

Canyon of the Dead, AZ 20–21, 21
Cape Cod, MA 258, 259, 260–61
Cape Cod 258
Cape Cod Windmill, MI 56, 56
Cape Flattery, WA 64, 66–67
Cape Mendocino, CA 10
Capitol, the, DC 50, 151
Carhenge, NE 199, 200
Carpenter Gothic style 153 see also Gothic (Revival) style, Victorian-era styles
Carpenters' Hall, PA 151
Carson National Forest, NM 146, 146–47
Casa del Desierto, CA 154
Cascade Mountain Range, WA 8, 10, 98, 226, 240, 241
Cassaday, KS 114–15, 117
Cathedral of Salamanca, Spain 45
Catskill Mountains, NY 229
cattle 8, 10, 29, 64, 93, 94, 97, 114–15, 117, 126, 126, 127, 155, 198–99, 199 see also ranches, ranching; rodeos
caves 20–21, 21
census, U.S. 151
Central City, CO 60–61, 63
Central Flyway 264
Chama, NM 212
Channel Islands, CA 226
Chapel of San Miguel, NM 92
Chappel Hill, TX 142, 142
Charleston, SC 18, 229
Charlottesville, VA 152
Châteauesque style 156
Chawse Indian Grinding Rock State Park, CA 196
Chesapeake Bay 18, 19, 229
Cheyenne, WY 154, 189, 189
Chicago, IL 8, 64, 71, 80–81, 83, 156, 157, 212, 214–15, 230: School of Architecture 156
Chihuahuan Desert 291
children 9, 10, 136, 164, 164, 165, 167, 168, 169, 180, 186, 212
Chimney Rock, NE 230
Christianity 91–92 see also individual denominations
Christmas 160, 160–61, 291
churches 8, 14, 32, 33, 33, 36–37, 38, 39, 40, 44, 45, 54, 90, 91, 92, 94, 156, 156, 209, 229 see also individual names
Civil War 59, 153–54
Clarence Buckingham Memorial Fountain, IL 80–81, 83
Cleveland, OH 8
Coca-Cola 218, 219
Cold War, the 157
College of William and Mary, VA 152
Colonial Parkway 56 see also National Parks
Colonial Williamsburg see Williamsburg, VA
Colorado 9, 63, 106, 212, 226, 230, 235
Colorado Plateau 230
Colorado River 230
Columbia, District of 48
Columbia Gorge, OR 269, 270
Columbia River 8, 10, 226
Columbus, OH 8
Columbus, Christopher 7
competitions 126, 166, 167, 167, 182, 183, 216–17, 217, 217
Confederation, Articles of 151
Congregational Church of Peru, MA 38, 40

Congress, Continental 151
Congress House, MD 151
Congress, U.S. 151
Connecticut 15, 17, 40, 117, 153
Connecticut River Valley 17
conquistadors 8, 92
Constitution, U.S. 17, 18, 151, 152
cooking 207
Cooperstown, NY 45, 45
Cornwallis, Lord 56
cottages 14, 19, 92, 153: French Colonial 19 see also homes, homesteads
Council Grove, KS 46, 46
Country magazine 94
courthouses 48, 48, 151 see also individual names
cowboys 8
crafts 26, 27, 28, 29, 40, 144, 144, 145, 155, 196, 196, 197, 197, 230
cranberries 140–41, 142
Crater Lake, OR 226, 238–39, 240
Crescent City, CA 155, 155
Crockett, Davy 91
Cumberland Gap 7
Cumbres and Toltec Scenic Railroad 212, 213
Dallas, TX 83, 84–85
dancing 172, 180, 180, 181, 182, 182, 183, 184, 185
Dare County, NC 258
Dare, Virginia 258
Davidson, Arthur 219
Davis, Bette 30
Daybreak Star Cultural Center, WA 182
Dearborn, MI 27, 29, 56
Death's Door Passage, WI 64
Death Valley, CA 8, 286, 286, 287
Deer Isle, ME 136, 138
Delaware 17, 153
Delaware River 229
Delgadillo family, the 208
Denali, AK 235, 235
Denio, NV 8
Department of the Interior, U.S. 291
deserts 230, 284–85, 286, 286, 287 see also individual names
DeSmet, Father Pierre Jean 240
Dessau, Germany 156
Detroit, MI 8
Devil's Den, PA 58, 59
Diamond Inn Bar, NV 8
Disney World, FL 172, 173
Divide Mountain, MT 240
dogs 8, 34–35, 146, 146–47, 160, 160–61, 166, 167, 189
Door County, WI 64
Douglas County, WI 264
Downing, Andrew Jackson 153
Dream Machine see Harley-Davidson
Dubuffet, Jean 11
Dutch Colonial style 8
Dutch East India Company 15
Early America at Work 94, 96
Early Modern architecture 156 see also Modern architecture
East Coast 8, 152, see also individual states
Eastern woodlands 7, 14
Edmund Fitzgerald, S.S. 226
Eiffel Tower, France 73
El Capitan, Yosemite, CA 230, 231
El Paso, TX 174
Empire State Building, NY 72, 73
England, English 18, 19, 152, 182, 199: Church of 14; Elizabethan 14
English style 8

Episcopal Church, St. Stephens, MA 39, 40
Erie Canal 8
Esplanade complex, MA 157
Europe, Europeans 7, 13, 15, 18, 19, 136, 152, 156
Everglades National Park, FL 225, 270, 270–71
Fachwerk style 17
Fairfax County, VA 152
Fair Oaks, CA 209
Fallasburg, MI 94, 95
farms 8, 16, 16–17, 40, 56, 91, 93, 94, 96, 97, 98, 98–99, 103, 106, 110, 111, 117, 128, 129, 137, 153, 199, 204, 229
Federal Hall, NY 151
Federal Reserve Act 264
Field, Marshall 264
fire departments 160: houses 160, 160–61; trucks 160, 161
Flat River, MI 94
Flint Hills, KS 103, 106
Florida 8, 18–19, 54, 92, 172, 225, 270
Florida Keys 225
flowers 116–17, 117, 128, 131, 133, 146, 226, 228, 235, 236–37, 250–51, 251: chrysanthemums 132, 133; daffodils 146, 149; lupines 235, 236–37; mustard 146, 148; paintbrush 235, 236–37; Pride of Madeira 250–51, 251; tulips 120–21, 124; valerian 235, 236–37
Fly Geyser, NV 274, 275
forests 8, 10, 16, 17, 228, 229, 268, 270, 272, 273, 290, 299 see also rainforests, trees
forts 92 see also individual names
Fort Charlotte, MN 21
Fort Mackinac, MI 46, 47
Fort Wood, NY 73
Founding fathers 10, 151, 152
fountains 80–81, 83 see also individual names
France, French 16, 19, 21, 40, 46, 73, 83, 91, 92, 93, 93, 157
Franciscan Order 92 see also Junipero Serra
Frankenmuth, MI 92, 92
Franklin, Benjamin 151
Fredericksburg, TX 174, 174–75
Fred Hartman Bridge, TX 83, 86–87
French Colonial style 19, 92
French, David Chester 151
French (Second) Empire style 45, 45, 156
Frijoles Canyon, NM 13
Furness, Frank 154
fur trade, traders 16, 19, 21, 180
Gallatin-Targhee National Forest, MT 290, 291
Garfield County, UT 199, 202–3
gas stations 199, 202–3
Gates of the Arctic, AK 228
Gateway Arch, MO 73, 74–75
Gateway to the West, the 8
George Washington Suspension Bridge, NY 79, 83
Georgia 18, 50, 53, 83, 264
Georgian style 152
German style 8
Germany, German 153, 156 see also individual names
Gettysburg Address 59
Gettysburg National Military Park, PA 58, 59, 59
geysers 274, 275, 276–77 see also individual names
Glacier Bay, AK 228

Glacier National Park, MT 230, 240, 242–43
gold 63, 155
Golden Gate Bridge, CA 8, 73, 78
Goliad State Park, TX 33
Gothic (Revival) style 38, 40, 91, 153 see also Carpenter Gothic style, Victorian-era styles
grain elevators 8, 97, 134, 134
Granby, CO 106
Grand Canyon, AZ 8, 230, 282, 283
Grand Central Terminal, NY 154, 154–55
Grand Coulee Dam 10
Grand Marais, MN 21
Grand Portage National Monument, MN 21, 22–23
Grand Tetons, WY 230, 240, 244–45
Grant, Cary 73
Grant Park, IL 80–81, 83
Great Fountain, WY 274, 276–77
Great Lakes, the 8, 9, 21, 152, 225, 230 see also individual names
Great Plains 7, 93, 134
Great Point, MA 258, 259
Great Smoky Mountain Range 229, 294–95, 299
Greek Revival style 48, 48, 54, 55, 152 see also Neoclassical style
Green Bay, WI 93
Greendale, WI 94
Greenfield Village, MI 26, 27, 28, 29, 29, 56, 56
Gregory, John 63
"Gregory's Lode" 63
Gropius, Walter 156–57
Guadalupe Mountains, TX 230
Gulf Coast 18, 262–63, 264
Gulf of Mexico 19, 225
Gulf Stream 225
Gunnison National Forest, CO 296–97, 299
Half Dome, Yosemite, CA 240, 240
Hamilton, Alexander 151
Hancock County, ME 136, 138
Hancock Shaker Village, MA 93
Hanelei River Valley, HI 122–23, 124
Harley-Davidson 219, 219
Harley, William 219
Hartford, CT 229
Harvard University, MA 157
Hawaii 124, 228, 251
Hawthorne, Nathaniel 16
Hayden, Michael 212
Hayden Valley, WY 240, 246–47
hex signs 16, 135, 135
hiking 9
Hinduism 155
Hingham, MA 14
Hoban, James 151
Hoh River Valley, WA 270, 273
Homer, AK 73
Homer Spit, AK 73, 76–77
homes, homesteads 8, 9, 14–19, 52, 91, 92, 96–97, 240, 244–45: bottle houses 150, 151; log cabins 153; Pfeiffer's, WY 240, 244–45; saltbox 17, 153, 153 see also cottages, town-houses
Homestead Act, the 154, 219
Hood River Valley, OR 117, 118, 119
Hook, Captain 204, 204
Hooker, Thomas 17
horses 93, 94, 94, 97, 136, 137, 144, 144, 160, 174–75, 198–99, 229
hot-air balloons 192, 193, 194

Hotel Coronado, CA 156
Hot Springs National Park, AR 229
houses see buildings, cottages, farms, homes, homesteads, townhouses
Houston, TX 10, 11, 83, 172, 172, 177, 178–79: Asian Festival 184, 184; Louisiana Street 10, 11; Power of Houston Exhibition 177; Ship Canal 83, 86–87
Hubbell Trading Post Historic Site, AZ 197, 197
Hudson, Henry 15
Hudson River Valley 15
Hutchinson, Anne 16
Ice Age 16, 228, 229, 240, 251
icons 209, 209
Idaho 134, 230
Illinois 64, 106, 128, 133, 157
Imperial County, CA 205, 205
Independence Day 155
Independence, Declaration of 13, 151, 152
Independence Hall, PA 151
India 155
Indiana 9, 16, 153
Indianapolis, IN 230
Intercourse, PA 133, 133
International style 157
Inyo National Forest, CA 274, 274
Iowa 251
Italianate style 156
Italy 152
Jackson, CA 9: Valley 97, 97
Jacksonville, CA 189, 190–91
jailhouses 45, 45
James River 18
Jamestown, VA 14, 54: harbor 21, 24–25
Japan, Japanese 48, 64
Jekyll Island, GA 264, 264–65
Jefferson Memorial, DC 151
Jefferson National Expansion Memorial Park, MO 73, 74–75
Jefferson, Thomas 18, 151, 152, 158–59, 160, 189
Jesuits 92
Jews, Judaism 16, 38, 40
Josephy, Alvin M. (Jr.) 7
Judeo-Christian heritage 91
Julia Pfeiffer Burns State Park, CA 251, 252–53
Jumping Frog Jubilee, CA 167, 167
Junipero Serra 92 see also Franciscan Order
Kachemak Bay, AK 73, 76–77
Kansas 46, 106, 117, 230
Kansas River 117
Karluk, AK 90, 91
Katmai National Park, AK 228
Kauai Island, HI 122–23, 124, 251, 282, 282
Kelly, Tom 151
Kenai Fords, AK 228
Kenai National Park, AK 73, 76–77
Kent, CT 112–13, 117, 153, 153
Kentucky 7, 229
Kilauea, HI 228
King's Canyon National Park, CA 288, 291
Knight, Leonard 205, 205
Kodiak Archipelago, AK 180
Kodiak Island, AK 90, 91, 124, 125, 180, 180
Konza Prairie Research Natural Area, KS 104, 106
Korean War 205
Lake Erie 9
Lake Huron 9, 46

Lake Michigan 9
Lake Superior 9, 21, 92, 226, 249, 251, 264, 266–67
Lakeview, OR 211, 211
Lancaster County, PA 136, 136, 151
La Porte, TX 83
La Salle County, IL 106, 108–9
Las Vegas, NV 207: Fremont Street 207
Latona Basin Fountain, France 83
Latrobe, Benjamin Henry 152
Le Corbusier 157
L'Enfant, Major Pierre Charles 151
Lexington, U.S.S. 212
Liberty Bell, WA 240, 241
Liberty, Statue of, NY 40, 40–41, 73, 73
Library of Congress, DC 152
lighthouses 15, 73, 225, 226, 226, 258, 258, 259, 260–61, 264, 266–67
Lincoln, Abraham 50, 59, 158–59, 160
Lincoln Memorial, DC 50–51, 151
Little Cottonwood Canyon, UT 64
Little League 168, 169 see also baseball
livestock see individual names
Lobster Festival, ME 136
Loehe, Wilhelm 92
logging 155
longhouses 14
Long Island, NY 15
Longs Peak, CO 226
Los Angeles, CA 8, 155
Louisiana / Louisiana Territory 19, 53, 54
"Lower 48" states 226, 228, 229
Lower Peninsula, MI 9
Lumahai Beach, HI 251, 255
Mackinac Island, MI 46, 47, 156
Madison, James 151
Madison River, WY 291, 291
Madonna, the 209, 209
mailboxes 194, 195, 195
Maine 136, 225, 300
Manhattan, KS 106
Manhattan Island, NY 15, 152, 152
marine life 225–26, 264
maritime heritage 15, 225
Markelius, Sven 157
Maroon Bells, CO 234, 235
Maryland 18, 19, 151, 152, 153
Massachusetts 14, 40, 45, 93, 142, 157, 258
Massachusetts Bay Colony 16, 17
Mata, Sri Daya 155
Mauna Loa, HI 228
Mayflower 14
Mazama Ridge, WA 235, 236–37
McWay Creek, CA 251, 252–53
meadows 10, 16
meetinghouses 14, 91 see also individual names
Mennonites 16, 93, 136 see also Amish
Mesa de Anguila, TX 289, 291
Mesquite Flats Sand Dunes, CA 286, 287
Methow Valley, WA 98, 100–1
Mexico, Mexican 8, 30, 91, 92, 181
Miami, FL 225
Michigan 8–9, 27, 29, 46, 56, 92, 94, 128, 156, 251
Middle Colonies 153
Midwest, the 7, 8, 91, 97, 128, 153, 230 see also individual place names
Mies van der Rohe, Ludwig 156–57
Milinkovitch, Miloje 209, 209
Miller, Frank 30
Miller, Henry 251

Milwaukee, WI 8
mining 63, 151, 154, 155
Miner's Castle, MI 249, 251
Minneapolis, MN 9, 230
Minnesota 21, 226
Mission Inn, CA 30, 30–31
Mission Revival style 92
missionaries, missions 46, 91–92, 240, 264, 291
Mississippi River 7, 8, 19, 73, 91, 92, 152, 225, 230, 248, 251
Missouri 46, 73, 93, 230
Missouri, U.S.S. 64
Mobile, AL 229
Modern architecture 156 see also Early Modern architecture
Monroe, WA 102, 106
Montana 9, 154, 230, 240, 291, 299
Monterey County, CA 250–51, 251, 252–53
Monticello, VA 152
Moody, John 96
Morgan, J.P. 264
Mormons 219, 291
Mormon Temple, UT 64, 70
Morro Rock, CA 82–83, 83
mountains 9, 73, 77–77, 227, 230, 231–45 see also individual names
Mount Hood, OR 117, 119, 226
Mount McKinley, AK 235, 235
Mount Mazama, OR 226
Mount Rainier, WA 226: National Park 235, 236–37
Mount Rushmore, SD 158–59
Mount St. Helens, WA 240
Mount Vernon, VA 152
Mount Washington, CA 155
Multnomah Falls, OR 269, 270
"Mummy Cave Ruins" see Canyon of the Dead
music 172, 173, 180, 180, 188, 188, 189, 189, 190–91
Mystic Seaport, CT 15
Nantucket Island, MA 17, 258, 259
Nassau Hall, NJ 151
National Archives Building, DC 151–52
National Historic Park, PA 229
National Mall, DC 48
National Parks 46, 56, 73, 225, 226, 228 see also under individual names
Native Americans 9, 13, 14, 16, 91–92, 182, 183, 230: Ahwahneechee 219; Algonkian 142; Alutiiq 180; Anasazi 13; Athabasca 235; Cherokee 14, 299; Chinook 270; Chippewa 46; Iroquois Nation 14; Makah 13; Miwok 196, 196; Navajo 21, 197, 197; Pueblo 13, 19; Seminole 18
Nauset Beach, MA 258, 260–61
Naval Academy, the United States, MD 19
Nebkota Railway Inc. 211
Nebraska 9, 199, 200, 201, 230
Neoclassical style 152, 152 see also Greek Revival style, Roman style
Netherlands, The 8, 15
Nevada 8, 151, 154, 194, 207, 274
New Amsterdam 15 see also New York City
New Deal 33
New England 14–17, 91, 93, 152, 155, 226, 229: Congregationalists 14, 229
New France 19 see also Canada
New Harmony, IN 153
New Hope, OH 16–17
New Jersey 15, 151, 153, 229

newlyweds 162–63, 164
New Mexico 13, 34, 46, 92, 142, 146, 194, 212
New Orleans, LA 10, 19, 54, 55, 92, 176, 177, 177, 229: French Quarter 10, 188, 188; Mardi Gras 176, 177, 177
Newport, RI 156
New Spain 33
New World 7, 8, 14, 15, 16, 92, 96, 258
New York 15, 45, 73, 117, 152, 156, 229
New York Battery, 4th, Memorial 58, 59
New York City, NY 8, 15, 72, 73, 79, 83, 151, 154, 154–55, 156, 157: Harbor 40, 40–41, 73; Stock Exchange, NY 152, 152 see also Manhattan
Nine Sisters, CA 83
Nixon, Pat 30
Nixon, Richard 30
North Bend, WA 182, 182
North Carolina 7, 8, 18, 156, 258, 299
North Dakota 9
Northwest, the 10, 17, 124, 226, 228, 291 see also individual place names
Nuestra Señora Del Espíritu Santo de Zuñiga Mission, TX 33, 33
Oak Alley, LA 52, 53
Oglethorpe, James 18
O'Hare International Airport, IL 212, 214–15
O'Hare, Lieutenant Commander Edward "Butch" 212
Ohio 9, 16
Ohio River 230
Olbrich, Josef Maria 156
Old Bedford Village, PA 40, 42–43
Old Court House, PA 151
Old Ship Church, Hingham, MA 14
Oligocene epoch 225
Olympic Mountains, WA 226
Olympic National Park, WA 226–27, 228, 251, 256–57, 270, 272, 273
Ontario, Canada 9
orchards 117, 118, 119 see also trees
Oregon 9, 10, 63, 117, 153, 211, 226, 270
Organ Pipe Cactus National Monument, AZ 284–85, 286
Oswego, NY 111, 117
Otsego County Jail, NY 45, 45
Otter Cliffs, ME 225, 225
Outer Banks, NC 8, 258
Ozark-Ouachita Highlands 230
Pacific 10, 225, 228: coast 7, 153, 226; Fleet 64; North 228; Northwest 7, 10, 13; South 251
Padre Island, TX 262–63, 264
Painted Desert, AZ 230
Palouse, WA 93, 93, 98, 98–99
Pantheon, the Italy 152
Paris, France 73
Pearland, TX 184, 185
Pemberton, John Styth 219
Penn, William 16, 17
Pennsylvania 13, 16–17, 40, 59, 97, 133, 135, 151, 153, 229
Pennsylvania Avenue, DC 151
Pennsylvania Station, PA 154
Pensacola, FL 18
Petrified Forest National Park, AZ 230
Philadelphia, PA 12, 13, 16, 151, 154, 229
Philadelphia & Reading Railroad 154
Pickett's Charge 59
Pike, Zebulon Montgomery 251
Pike's Peak, IA 248, 251
Pilgrims, the 14, 142
Pine Grove, OR 117

pioneers 10, 13, 199 see also settlers
Pittsburgh, PA 154
plains 9, 199, 230 see also individual names
plantations 18, 19, 53, 152
Plymouth, CA 160, 161
Plymouth, MA 14, 142
Point of Arches, WA 251, 256–57
Pollock, Jackson 10
Pope, Andrew Jackson 155
Porterville, CA 146, 148
Port Gamble, WA 155
Portland, OR 10, 153, 226
Potomac River 152
prairies 9, 13, 93, 97, 104, 105, 106, 117, 219, 220–21, 230
Princeton, NJ 151
Protestant 18: Reformation 136
Providence, RI 16, 229
Pueblo style 19, 34, 92
Puget Sound 10
Pulitzer, Joseph 264
Pulpit, The, UT 291, 292–93
pumpkins 128, 129, 132, 133, 142, 143
Puritans 14, 16, 17: meetinghouses 14
Quakers 14, 16, 18
Quebec, Canada 19
Queen Anne Revival style 156
quilts 133, 133, 155
Racetrack Playa, CA 286, 286
railroads 8, 13, 63, 97, 134, 152, 154, 155, 212, 213, 230: companies 154, 211; depots 154; lines 154; locomotives 152, 210, 211, 213; stations 91, 154, 154 see also individual names
rainforests 226, 228 see also forests, trees
ranching 94, 97, 98, 100–1, 146, 148, 274 see also agriculture, cattle, rodeos, rural America
Rancho de Taos, NM 92
Reading Terminal, PA 12, 13
Reagan, Nancy 30
Reagan, Ronald 30
Redmond Festival, WA 94, 94
Red Rocks Lakes National Wildlife Refuge, MT 298, 299
reefs 225
Refugio, TX 160, 160–61
Reinders, Jim 199
religions see under individual names
Renaissance style 13
Reno, NV 194
Reunion Tower, TX 83, 84–85
Revolutionary War 17, 40, 46, 151, 152
Rheinland, Germany 16
Rhode Island 16, 156
Rhyolite, NV 150, 151
Rich, Charles C. 219
Richardson, Henry Hobson 45, 154
Rich County, UT 219, 220–21
Richmond, VA 152
Richmondtown Restoration, NY 15
Ridgefield, CT 39, 40: Battle of 40
Rio Grande 291
Riverside, CA 30, 30–31
roads 6, 13, 97 see also Route 66
Roanoke Island, NC 258
Roark Bluff, AR 300
Robertson, Robert H. 93
Rockefeller, John D. (Jr.) 152
Rockefeller, William 264
Rockport, ME 136, 139
Rocky Mountains 7, 8, 9, 10, 98, 230: National Park, CO 226, 227
rodeos 94, 126, 126, 127 see also cattle, ranching
Roman Catholic Church 14, 18

Romanesque see Roman style
Roman style 44, 45, 152 see also Neoclassical style
Rome, Italy 152
Roosevelt, Franklin D. 33, 212, 235
Roosevelt, Theodore 158–59, 160
Root, Wellborn 156
Rotunda, the, VA 152
Route 66 207: Historic Route 66 Society 208
rural America 90–149, 230 see also agriculture
Russian Orthodoxy 91
Saarinen, Eero 73
Sacramento, CA 181, 181
Saginaw Valley, MI 92
St. Anthony, ID 134, 134
St. Augustine, FL 8, 18, 54, 54, 92
St. Elmo's fire 73
St. Louis, MO 8, 73, 74–75, 93, 156, 230
St. Mary Lake, MT 240, 242–43
Salem, MA 14
Salinas, MI 128, 128
Salt Lake City, UT 64, 70
Salvation Mountain, CA 205
San Antonio, TX 32, 33, 91, 91, 92, 230
San Antonio de Valero, TX 92
San Fernando Cathedral, TX 32, 33
San Francisco, CA 8, 73, 78, 156, 228 Bay 8, 64, 68–69
San Francisco de Asis, NM 92
San Francisco de Espada, TX 92
San Jacinto, Battle of 83
Santa Elena Canyon, TX 291
Sante Fe, NM 92, 154, 230: Railroad 154; Trail 46
Savannah, GA 18, 53, 53, 229
scarecrows 142, 142, 143
Scarlet Letter, The 16
Schenectady, NY 15
schools 91, 229
Scott's Bluff National Monument, NE 199, 201
sea stacks 64, 66–67, 226
Seattle, WA 10, 83, 88–89, 153, 182, 183, 226
Secessionist movement, Austria 156
Self-Realization Fellowship 155
Seligman, AZ 208, 208
Seminary Ridge, PA 59, 59
settlers 9: Acadian 19; African American 154; Asian 154; Cajun 19; Creole 19; Dutch 8, 15; Eastern European 230; English 8, 14, 18, 54, 258; French 19; French Canadian 8, 19; French Huguenot 18; German 8, 17, 18, 92, 96, 97, 135, 153, 154, 230; Japanese 154–55; Mexican 8; Mormon 219; Russian 124, 180; Scandinavian 8, 230; Scots-Irish 17, 18, 153; Swedish 8, 17, 96, 153 see also pioneers
Seville Cathedral, Spain 64
Shaconage 299
Shakers 14–15, 93
Shaniko, OR 63, 63
sheep 63, 97, 146, 146–47, 197
Shelburne Farms, VT 93
Shenandoah National Park, VA 232–33, 235
Shields Tavern, VA 27, 27
Shintoism 91
ships: shipwrecks 64, 66–67 see also boats and individual names
Shi-Shi Beach, WA 251, 256–57
Siberia 7, 124
Sierra Nevada, CA 291

silos 97, 102, 106, 112–13, 117
Sinatra, Frank 64
Skagit Valley, WA 120–21, 124, 146, 149
skiing 9, 63
skyscrapers 11, 64, 71, 72, 73, 84–85, 88–89, 156, 178–79 see also individual names
"Sky's the Limit, The" 212, 214–15
slavery 18, 153 see also Africa, Africans
Sleepless in Seattle 73
Sloane, Eric 96
Smith, Jedediah 9
Smith, William 207
Smithsonian Institution 151
Snowmass Wilderness, CO 234, 235
soccer 169, 169
Society of Jesus see Jesuits
Soleduck Valley, WA 270, 272
South Carolina 18, 19
South Dakota 9, 160, 225, 230
South Pass 9
South Rim, AZ 282
Spain, Spanish 7, 18, 19, 21, 34, 54, 64, 91, 92
Spanish style 8, 92
Split Rock Lighthouse State Park, MN 226, 226
sports see individual names
Sri Meenakshi Temple, TX 184, 185
Standard, VT 36–37, 40
Stars and Stripes, the 12, 13, 174, 174–75
State Capitol, VA 152
Staten Island, NY 15
Strait of Juan de Fuca 10
Straits of Mackinac 9
Strong City, KS 196
Sturgeon Bay, WI 64, 64–65
Sullivan, Louis 156
Supreme Court Building, DC 48, 48
Sutter Creek, CA 124
Sweden, Swedish 8, 157
Switzerland, Swiss 16, 157
Syracuse, NY 110, 117
Talbot, Frederic 155
Taos, NM 230: Pueblo 34, 34–35
Telluride, CO 62, 63
Temple of Sinawara, the, UT 291
Tennessee 299
Texas 33, 83, 91, 92, 142, 160, 172, 174, 177, 184, 225, 230, 264, 291
Thai dancing 184, 184
Thanksgiving 142: parades 172, 172
Thoreau, Henry David 258
Tidal Basin, DC 48, 49, 151
Tidewater, the 18, 229
tobacco 17, 18, 97
Toketee 268, 270
Tokyo, Japan 48
Toltec Gorge 212
townhouses 8, 15, 53, 53, 55, 156 see also homes, homesteads
trailers 205, 205
trappers 9, 16
Travis, William 91
trees 96–97, 230, 272, 292–93, 294–301: aspen 296–97, 299; Bristlecone pine 274, 274; cedar 97; cherry 48, 49; chestnut 97; cottonwood 228; General Grant Redwood 291; giant sequoia 8, 288, 291; Hala 251, 254; hickory 97; maple 270, 273; Methuselah 274; Norfolk pine 230; oak 52, 53, 97; palm 146, 148, 251, 254; pear 117, 118, 119; pine 97, 230, 240, 240; Ponderosa pine 10; poplar 102, 106; sugar maple 300, 301; vine maple

228; yellow birch 300, 301 see also forests, orchards, rainforests
Trinity Church, MA 44, 45
Trost Feed & Seed Company 134, 134
Truxton, AZ 207, 207
Tudor Revival style 18
Twain, Mark 167
Umpqua National Forest, OR 268, 270
Union Pacific Railroad 154
United Indians of All Tribes Foundation 182 see also Native Americans
United Nations complex, NY 157
University of Virginia, VA 152
Upper Geyser Basin, WY 229
Upper Peninsula, MI 9
Utah 64, 199, 219, 230, 282, 291
Vanderbilt family 156
Vedic dancers 184, 185
Vegas Vic 207
vehicles, motor 8, 97, 134, 161, 162–63, 186, 187, 199, 200, 204, 204, 211, 211, 219, 219, 220–21
Verela, Jesús 146, 146–47
Vermont 40, 93, 96
Versailles, France 83
Victorian-era styles 153 see also Gothic (Revival) style
vineyards 97, 116–17, 117, 124 see also wine and individual names
Virginia 14, 17, 18, 21, 27, 56, 93, 152, 235
volcanoes 83, 226, 228, 240, 251 see also individual names
wagons 46, 46, 64, 199, 201
Waikoko Bay, HI 251, 254
Wall Street, NY 15
War Eagle Creek, AR 128, 130
War Eagle Mill, AR 128, 130
War of 1812 151
Washington 10, 64, 93, 94, 95, 98, 106, 124, 149, 153, 155, 169, 182, 226, 235, 240, 251, 270
Washington, DC 48, 48, 49, 50, 50–51, 151–52
Washington, George 56, 151, 152, 158–59, 160
Washington Island 64
Washington Monument, DC 48, 49, 151
Washoe County, NV 274
Waumei Canyon, HI 282, 282

Webb, Lila Vanderbilt 93
Webb, William Seward 93
Wendover, NV 206, 207
Wendover Will 206, 207
West, the 93, 97, 134, 153, 226 see also individual place names
West Coast 154, 155 see also individual states
West Indies 19
West Yarmouth, MA 140–41, 142
White House, the, DC 151
White Mountains, CA 274
Whitman County, WA 98, 98–99
Williams, Roger 16
Williamsburg, VA 21, 24–25, 27, 93, 152
Wilson, Everett B. 94
Wilson, Vincent (Jr.) 151
wind farms 228, 228
windmills 16–17, 56, 56, 93
wine 97, 117 see also vineyards
Winthrop, WA 98
Wisconsin 9, 64, 93, 94, 264
Wisconsin Point Lighthouse, WI 264, 266–67
Wolfe, Thomas 230
World War II 64, 156, 212
Wrangal-St. Elias, AK 228
Wren Building, VA 152
Wright, Frank Lloyd 156
Wrigley Building, IL 64, 71
Württemberg, Germany 153
Wyoming 9, 154, 162–63, 164, 189, 229, 230, 240, 291
Yadkin River 7
"Yankee peddlers" 17
Yellowstone National Park, WY 46, 229, 229, 230, 240, 246–47, 274, 276–77, 278, 279
Yellowstone River, WY 230, 240, 246–47
yoga 155
Yogananda, Paramahansa 155
York, PA 151
York County Court House, PA 151
Yorktown, VA 56, 57
Yosemite National Park, CA 219, 222–23, 230, 231, 240, 240
Young, Brigham 219
Zion National Park, UT 291, 292–93
Zuñiga, Baltásar de 33

ACKNOWLEDGMENTS AND PHOTO CREDITS

The publisher would like to thank all who assisted in the production of this book, including everyone who was photographed and/or whose property or work appear in these pages; Clare Haworth-Maden for compiling the index; the Boston Fire Department; and countless individuals for information provided on their websites. Particular thanks are due to the photographers listed below for permission to reproduce the photographs on the following pages: © **Larry Angier**: 13, 20–21, 34–35, 97, 116–17, 134, 146–47, 150, 156, 257, 162–63, 167, 168, 196, 198–99, 200, 205, 207, 208, 209, 213, 222–23, 228, 231, 274; © **Mary Liz Austin**: 119, 138, 139, 158–59, 236–37, 252–53, 255, 268, 269, 284–85, endpapers; © **Kindra Clineff**: 36–37, 259, 260–61; © **Ed Cooper**: 15, 22–23, 45, 60–61, 62, 63, 66–67, 76–77, 82–83, 95, 110, 111, 155, 224, 225, 226, 227, 234, 235, 240, 248, 249, 270–71; © **Terry Donnelly**: 1, 58, 59, 88–89, 98–99, 108–109, 118, 122–23, 130–31, 132, 229, 232–33, 238–39, 250–51, 254, 262–63, 264–65, 266–67, 276–77, 280–81, 282, 286, 287, 288, 289, 292–93, 294–95, 296–97, 300, 301; © **Robert Drapala**: 12; © **Carolyn Fox**: 2, 6, 8, 9, 30–31, 68–69, 106–107, 124, 144, 145, 148, 161, 164, 166, 170–71, 181, 187, 189, 193, 194, 195, 197, 201, 202–203, 204, 206, 210, 211, 212, 216–17, 220–21, 275; © **A. Blake Gardner**: 258; © **Rudi Holnsteiner**: 11, 24–25, 32, 33, 40–41, 42–43, 53, 74–75, 84–85, 86–87, 92, 133, 136, 140–41, 142, 143, 160–61, 172, 174–75, 176, 177, 178–79, 184, 185, 186, 192, 219; © **Wolfgang Kaehler**: 3, 10, 19, 26–27, 28, 29, 46, 47, 50–51, 54, 56, 57, 64–65, 70, 71, 78, 79, 80–81, 90, 91, 93, 94, 96, 100–101, 102, 103, 104, 105, 114–15, 120–21, 125, 126, 127, 149, 165, 169, 173, 180, 182, 183, 188, 190–91, 214–15, 217, 218, 241, 241–43, 244–45, 246–47, 256–57, 272, 273, 278, 279, 283, 290, 291, 298–99; © **Balthazar Korab**: 38, 44, 52, 55, 128, 129; © **Charles J. Ziga**: 14, 16–17, 39, 48, 49, 72, 73, 112–13, 135, 137, 152, 153; 154–155.